MATH Trailblazers®

A BALANCED MATHEMATICS PROGRAM INTEGRATING SCIENCE AND LANGUAGE ARTS

Unit Resource Guide
Unit 2

Strategies:
An Assessment Unit

THIRD EDITION

KENDALL/HUNT PUBLISHING COMPANY
4050 Westmark Drive   Dubuque, Iowa 52002

A TIMS® Curriculum
University of Illinois at Chicago

UIC The University of Illinois at Chicago

The original edition was based on work supported by the National Science Foundation under grant No. MDR 9050226 and the University of Illinois at Chicago. Any opinions, findings, and conclusions or recommendations expressed in this publication are those of the author(s) and do not necessarily reflect the views of the granting agencies.

Letter Home

Strategies: An Assessment Unit

Date: _____

Dear Family Member:

Your child will study addition and subtraction facts throughout the year. The treatment of the basic math facts in *Math Trailblazers®* differs from traditional textbooks. We encourage students to use strategies to solve math fact problems, rather than rely on rote memorization. Researchers have found that this approach increases learning and retention.

In this unit, your child's work on the subtraction facts includes discussions of strategies, work with flash cards, and a game.

- **Activities.** Students will find a need to learn the facts as they use them to solve problems in labs and activities.
- **Flash Cards.** Your child will work with flash cards that are organized into eight small groups of facts. Help your child practice at home with the flash cards for Groups 1 and 2.
- **Games.** Students practice the facts while playing games. Encourage your child to show you these games or challenge him or her to play a game with you.
- **Daily Practice and Problems.** Students solve problems that review or practice math concepts and skills including periodic practice with small groups of facts.

Children learn math facts as they play *Nine, Ten*.

As you work with your child on the math facts, ask him or her to describe the strategies used to find the answers.

The mathematics curriculum is designed so students can work toward learning the basic math facts while at the same time learning more complex mathematics. In this way, math remains meaningful to the student. During the first half of third grade, students review the subtraction facts and learn to use strategies for the multiplication facts.

I look forward to working together with you and your child.

Sincerely,

_____

Carta al hogar

Estrategias: Una unidad de evaluación

Fecha: _____

Estimado miembro de familia:

Su hijo/a estudiará conceptos básicos acerca de la suma y de la resta durante todo el año. En *Math Trailblazers®* los conceptos básicos de la suma y de la resta se enseñan de una manera diferente a los libros tradicionales. Animamos a los estudiantes a usar estrategias para resolver problemas relacionados con los conceptos matemáticos básicos en lugar de recurrir a la memorización. Los investigadores han descubierto que este enfoque aumenta el aprendizaje y la retención.

En esta unidad, el trabajo de su hijo/a con las restas básicas incluye hablar sobre estrategias, trabajar con tarjetas y jugar un juego.

- **Actividades.** Los estudiantes descubrirán la necesidad de aprender los conceptos básicos cuando los usan para resolver problemas en investigaciones y actividades.
- **Tarjetas.** Su hijo/a trabajará con tarjetas que han sido clasificadas en ocho pequeños grupos de operaciones básicas. Ayude a su hijo/a a practicar en casa con las tarjetas de los grupos 1 y 2.
- **Juegos.** Los estudiantes practicarán los conceptos básicos mientras juegan. Pídale a su hijo/a que le muestre estos juegos o desafíelo a que juegue un juego con usted.
- **Práctica diaria y problemas.** Los estudiantes resuelven problemas cuya solución requiere repasar o practicar conceptos y habilidades matemáticos incluyendo la práctica periódica con grupos pequeños de conceptos básicos.

Los estudiantes aprenden los conceptos básicos mientras juegan un juego llamado *Nueve, diez.*

Mientras usted trabaja junto a su hijo/a para ayudar en el aprendizaje de estos conceptos matemáticos, pídale que describa las estrategias usadas para hallar las respuestas.

El programa de matemáticas está diseñado para que los estudiantes puedan trabajar para aprender los conceptos matemáticos básicos mientras aprenden al mismo tiempo conceptos matemáticos más complejos. De esta manera, las matemáticas tendrán sentido para el estudiante. Durante la primera mitad de tercer grado, los estudiantes repasarán los conceptos básicos de la resta y aprenderán a usar estrategias para las tablas de multiplicación.

Será un placer trabajar con usted y con su hijo/a.

Atentamente,

Table of Contents

Unit 2
Strategies: An Assessment Unit

Unit 2

Outline
Strategies: An Assessment Unit

Unit Summary

Estimated Class Sessions

12

This unit provides baseline measures about a broad range of students' mathematical understandings and competencies. The activities include opportunities for teachers to assess students' arithmetic skills, mathematical concepts, and abilities to solve problems and communicate solutions.

Students investigate patterns in addition and subtraction sentences for two of the activities. Portfolios of student work are organized during this unit. The information from the formal assessment instruments in this unit will complement samples of student work to provide a comprehensive and balanced picture of students' mathematical understandings near the beginning of the school year.

The unit also includes the Adventure Book, *Yü the Great,* which introduces students to magic squares. The DPP for this unit reviews the subtraction facts for Groups 1 and 2.

Major Concept Focus

- addition and subtraction facts practice
- subtraction facts review for Groups 1 and 2
- number sense
- *Adventure Book:* origin of magic squares
- magic squares
- collecting, organizing, and graphing data
- bar graphs
- interpreting graphs
- Student Rubric: *Knowing*
- communicating problem-solving solutions
- assessment of problem solving

Pacing Suggestions

Students' fluency with the addition and subtraction facts and their abilities to solve problems and communicate their reasoning will determine how quickly the class can proceed through this unit. The following recommendations will help you adapt the unit to your students' needs.

- In Lesson 5 *Subtraction Facts Strategies* and Lesson 7 *Assessing the Subtraction Facts,* students assess their fluency with the subtraction facts and begin a systematic review of facts they need to study. The subtraction facts are divided into eight groups of nine facts each. In this unit they review the subtraction facts in Groups 1 and 2. Work with the remaining groups of facts is distributed throughout the Daily Practice and Problems and Home Practice in each unit. All students should continue learning new concepts and skills while working on the facts.

- The math facts program is closely linked to the recommended schedule for teaching lessons. Therefore, classrooms that differ significantly from the suggested pacing will need to make accommodations to ensure that students receive a consistent program of math facts practice and assessment throughout the year. The *Grade 3 Facts Resource Guide* outlines a schedule for the study of the subtraction and multiplication facts in classrooms that move much more slowly through lessons than is recommended in the Lesson Guides. For more information, see the *Grade 3 Facts Resource Guide* and the TIMS Tutor: *Math Facts* in the *Teacher Implementation Guide.*

Assessment Indicators

Use the following Assessment Indicators and the *Observational Assessment Record* that follows the Background section in this unit to assess students on key ideas.

A1. Can students use strategies to add and subtract?

A2. Can students make and interpret bar graphs?

A3. Can students collect, organize, graph, and analyze data?

A4. Can students use patterns in data tables and graphs to make predictions and solve problems?

A5. Can students communicate mathematical reasoning verbally and in writing?

Unit Planner

KEY: SG = Student Guide, DAB = Discovery Assignment Book, AB = Adventure Book, URG = Unit Resource Guide, DPP = Daily Practice and Problems, HP = Home Practice (found in Discovery Assignment Book), and TIG = Teacher Implementation Guide.

	Lesson Information	Supplies	Copies/Transparencies
Lesson 1 **Addition Facts Strategies** URG Pages 28–38 SG Pages 14–15 DAB Pages 25–27 DPP A–D *Estimated Class Sessions* **2**	**Activity** Students partition numbers, rearrange addends, and use strategies with addition facts. **Math Facts** DPP Bit A provides practice with math facts. **Homework** 1. Assign the *Switch It!* Homework Page in the *Discovery Assignment Book*. 2. Assign the *Calculator Explorations* Homework Page. **Assessment** Students complete the *Calculator Challenges* Assessment Page.	• 40 connecting cubes per student pair • 1 calculator per student pair	• 1 copy of *Calculator Challenges* URG Page 36 per student • 1 transparency of *Calculator Explorations* DAB Page 27, optional
Lesson 2 **Spinning Sums** URG Pages 39–53 SG Pages 16–18 DAB Pages 29–31 DPP E–H HP Parts 1–2 *Estimated Class Sessions* **2**	**Activity** Students spin two spinners to randomly generate addition sentences. They record these facts in a data table and graph the number of times they spin each sum. **Math Facts** DPP Bit E provides practice with math facts. Parts 1 and 2 of the Home Practice provide addition and subtraction practice. **Homework** Assign Home Practice Parts 1 and 2. **Assessment** Use the *Observational Assessment Record* to note students' abilities to use strategies to add quickly and accurately.	• 1 clear plastic spinner (or pencils with paper clips) per student group • 1 blank transparency, optional	• 1 copy of *Horizontal Bar Graph* URG Page 50 per student group • 1 transparency of *Spinners 2–9* DAB Page 29 • 1 transparency of *Spinning Sums Data Table* DAB Page 31 • 1 transparency of *Horizontal Bar Graph* URG Page 50 • 1 copy of *Observational Assessment Record* URG Pages 15–16 to be used throughout this unit
Lesson 3 **Yü the Great A Chinese Legend** URG Pages 54–63 AB Pages 12–25 DPP I–J HP Part 3–4 *Estimated Class Sessions* **1**	**Adventure Book** This story introduces Lo-shu, a pattern on the back of a turtle, which was the first magic square. **Homework** Assign Parts 3 and 4 of the Home Practice in the *Discovery Assignment Book* for homework.		

	Lesson Information	Supplies	Copies/ Transparencies
Lesson 4 **Magic Squares** URG Pages 64–72 SG Pages 19–21 DAB Page 33 DPP K–L *Estimated Class Sessions* **1**	**Activity** Students solve magic squares to develop problem-solving and addition skills. **Math Facts** Task L is a line math puzzle. **Homework** Assign the homework in the *Student Guide.*	• scissors • calculators	• blank transparency • 1 transparency of *Digits* DAB Page 33
Lesson 5 **Subtraction Facts Strategies** URG Pages 73–80 SG Pages 22–27 DAB Page 35 DPP M–P *Estimated Class Sessions* **2**	**Activity** Students begin a review of subtraction facts through the use of strategies. **Math Facts** DPP items N and O provide practice with math facts. **Homework** Students play *Nine, Ten* at home. **Assessment** 1. Use DPP Task N to assess students' understanding of the Magic Square activity. 2. Use the *Observational Assessment Record* to note students' use of strategies to subtract.	• 2 clear spinners (or pencils and paper clips) per student pair and 2 for the teacher	• 1 transparency of *Spinners 11–18 and 9–10* DAB Page 35
Lesson 6 **Spinning Differences** URG Pages 81–92 DAB Page 29 DPP Q–T *Estimated Class Sessions* **2**	**Assessment Activity** In this assessment activity, students spin two spinners and randomly generate subtraction sentences to find the most common difference. **Math Facts** DPP items Q, R, and T provide practice with math facts. **Assessment** Use the *TIMS Multidimensional Rubric* to score the activity, focusing on the Knowing dimension.	• 2 clear spinners (or pencil-paper clip substitute) per student pair	• 1 copy of *Spinning Differences* URG Page 90 per student • 1 copy of *Spinning Differences Data Table* URG Page 91 per student • 1 copy of *Horizontal Bar Graph* URG Page 50 per student • 1 transparency or poster of Student Rubric: *Knowing* TIG, Assessment section • 1 copy of *TIMS Multidimensional Rubric* TIG, Assessment section • 1 transparency of *Spinners 2–9* DAB Page 29, optional

(Continued)

Lesson 7

Assessing the Subtraction Facts

URG Pages 93–104
DAB Pages 37–43

DPP U–V

Estimated Class Sessions

1

Assessment Activity
Students are introduced to the *Subtraction Flash Cards* and the *Subtraction Facts I Know* chart as a means of self-assessment.

Math Facts
DPP Bit U provides practice with addition facts.

Homework
Students take home the flash cards for Group 1 and Group 2 to practice the subtraction facts with a family member.

• 1 envelope for storing flash cards per student

• 1 copy of *Information for Parents: Grade 3 Math Facts Philosophy* URG Pages 13–14 per student

• 1 back-to-back copy of *Subtraction Flash Cards: Group 1* URG Pages 101–102 per student, optional

• 1 back-to-back copy of *Subtraction Flash Cards: Group 2* URG Pages 103–104 per student, optional

• 1 transparency of *Subtraction Facts I Know* DAB Page 43, optional

Lesson 8

Number Sense with Dollars and Cents

URG Pages 105–111
SG Pages 28–29

DPP W–X

Estimated Class Sessions

1

Activity
Students solve word problems from a list of items and prices.

Assessment
1. Use the *Observational Assessment Record* to document students' abilities to verbally communicate mathematical reasoning.
2. Transfer appropriate assessment documentation from the Unit 2 *Observational Assessment Record* to students' *Individual Assessment Record Sheets*.

• 1 copy of *Individual Assessment Record Sheet* TIG Assessment section per student, previously copied for use throughout the year

Connections

A current list of literature and software connections is available at *www.mathtrailblazers.com*. You can also find information on connections in the *Teacher Implementation Guide* Literature List and Software List sections.

Literature Connections

Suggested Titles

- Murphy, Frank. *Ben Franklin and the Magic Squares.* Random House, Inc., New York, 2000.
- "The Straw, the Coal, and the Bean" from *The Complete Grimm's Fairy Tales.* Random House, Inc., New York, 1992. (Lesson 3)

Software Connections

- *Graphers* is a data graphing tool appropriate for young students.
- *Ice Cream Truck* develops problem solving, money skills, and arithmetic operations.
- *Math Concepts One . . . Two . . . Three!* provides exploration and practice with the four operations including work with magic squares.
- *Mighty Math Calculating Crew* poses short answer questions about number operations, 3-dimensional shapes, and money skills.
- *Money Challenge* provides practice with money.
- *Number Facts Fire Zapper* provides practice with number facts in an arcade-like game.
- *Numbers Recovered* provides practice with bar graphs.
- *Penny Pot* provides practice with counting coins.

Teaching All Math Trailblazers Students

Math Trailblazers lessons are designed for students with a wide range of abilities. The lessons are flexible and do not require significant adaptation for diverse learning styles or academic levels. However, when needed, lessons can be tailored to allow students to engage their abilities to the greatest extent possible while building knowledge and skills.

To assist you in meeting the needs of all students in your classroom, this section contains information about some of the features in the curriculum that allow all students access to mathematics. For additional information, see the Teaching the *Math Trailblazers* Student: Meeting Individual Needs section in the *Teacher Implementation Guide.*

Differentiation Opportunities in this Unit

Games

Use games to promote or extend understanding of math concepts and to practice skills with children who need more practice.

- *Nine, Ten* from Lesson 5 *Subtraction Facts Strategies*

Journal Prompts

Journal prompts provide opportunities for students to explain and reflect on mathematical problems. They can help both students who need practice explaining their ideas and students who benefit from answering higher order questions. Students with various learning styles can express themselves using pictures, words, and sentences. Teachers can alter journal prompts to suit students' ability levels. The following lessons contain a journal prompt:

- Lesson 2 *Spinning Sums*
- Lesson 4 *Magic Squares*
- Lesson 5 *Subtraction Facts Strategies*

DPP Challenges

DPP Challenges are items from the Daily Practice and Problems that usually take more than fifteen minutes to complete. These problems are more thought-provoking and can be used to stretch students' problem-solving skills. The following lessons have DPP Challenges in them:

- DPP Challenge D from Lesson 1 *Addition Facts Strategies*
- DPP Challenge H from Lesson 2 *Spinning Sums*
- DPP Challenges R and T from Lesson 6 *Spinning Differences*
- DPP Challenge V from Lesson 7 *Assessing the Subtraction Facts*

Extensions

Use extensions to enrich lessons. Many extensions provide opportunities to further involve or challenge students of all abilities. Take a moment to review the extensions prior to beginning this unit. Some extensions may require additional preparation and planning. The following lessons contain extensions:

- Lesson 1 *Addition Facts Strategies*
- Lesson 4 *Magic Squares*
- Lesson 5 *Subtraction Facts Strategies*

Background
Strategies: An Assessment Unit

Baseline Assessment

This unit is a collection of activities that provides information about students' mathematical knowledge. It has several major goals: The first is to provide a framework for the ongoing development of students' number sense and knowledge of the basic math facts. The activities, games, and Daily Practice and Problems will address these topics throughout the year.

A second goal is to provide lessons that allow you to assess students' mathematical knowledge. This unit provides opportunities for both formal and informal assessment and includes a balance of short, medium-length, and extended activities. Students will begin collecting materials to keep in their portfolios. Each student will add to his or her portfolio throughout the year as a record of progress. See the TIMS Tutor: *Portfolios* in the *Teacher Implementation Guide* for information on the use of assessment portfolios.

Rubrics

Student work is also assessed using the *TIMS Multidimensional Rubric*. In addition to the teacher's version of the rubric, there are Student Rubrics to ·help students reflect upon mathematics as they begin their work and as they revise it. In this unit, students are introduced to the Student Rubric: *Knowing*. Later units will introduce the other two rubrics, *Solving* and *Telling*. See the Assessment section of the *Teacher Implementation Guide* for a discussion of the rubrics.

Journals

This is a good unit for students to begin math journals. Math journals are a rich assessment source. Many of the journal prompts in the Lesson Guides elicit information about students' understanding of

specific concepts, their abilities to communicate this understanding verbally, and their attitudes about mathematics. See the TIMS Tutor: *Journals* for more information.

Math Facts

"Knowing basic number combinations—the single-digit addition and multiplication pairs, and their counterparts for subtraction and division—is essential. Equally essential is computational fluency—having and using efficient and accurate methods for computing. Fluency might be manifested in using a combination of mental strategies and jottings on paper or using an algorithm with paper and pencil, particularly when the numbers are large, to produce accurate results quickly. Regardless of the particular method used, students should be able to explain their method, understand that many methods exist, and see the usefulness of methods that are efficient, accurate, and general."

From the National Council of Teachers of Mathematics *Principles and Standards for School Mathematics,* p. 32, 2000.

Lessons 5–7 and the Daily Practice and Problems (DPP) for Unit 2 begin a yearlong systematic math facts program. It builds upon similar work in Grade 2 that practiced and assessed the addition and subtraction facts. DPP items in Units 2–10 provide review and assessment of small groups of subtraction facts. See the Daily Practice and Problems Guide for this unit for the distribution of the subtraction facts review and assessment in the DPP. All the subtraction facts are assessed in Unit 10. Students study the multiplication facts using a similar process in Units 11–20. See the

Daily Practice and Problems Guide for Units 3 and 11 for the distribution of the review and assessment of the multiplication facts.

The research that contributed to the National Council of Teachers of Mathematics *Principles and Standards for School Mathematics* and the National Research Council's *Adding It Up* has informed the structure of the math facts strand in *Math Trailblazers*. For a detailed explanation of the strand, see the TIMS Tutor: *Math Facts* in the *Teacher Implementation Guide* and the *Grade 3 Facts Resource Guide*. Also see the *Information for Parents: Grade 3 Math Facts Philosophy* that immediately follows this Background.

Subtraction Facts Strategies

As stated in *Mathematics for the Young Child*, "Encouraging children to use efficient strategies to derive unknown facts before drill is better than 'premature drill'. . . and doing so increases both initial learning and retention." (Thornton, 1990, p. 134)

Throughout the curriculum, students are encouraged to invent their own strategies and to share their thinking with one another. However, particular emphasis is given to the strategies described below.

Counting Strategies

Counting up is most efficient when the numbers are close together, as in $11 - 8$ or $30 - 28$. To subtract 8 from 11, students start at the lower number (8) and keep track of how many they count to get to 11 (9, 10, 11).

Counting back is most efficient when the number to be subtracted is small, as in $11 - 3$ or $30 - 2$. In this case, students start at the higher number (11), count backward the amount of the lower number (3), and find the number he or she stops at (8).

Using Doubles

If students are comfortable with doubles, e.g., $8 + 8 = 16$ and $6 + 6 = 12$, they can use these facts to learn "half-doubles" as well: $16 - 8 = 8$ and $12 - 6 = 6$. These facts can then be used to figure out close facts, such as $13 - 6 = 7$ and $15 - 8 = 7$.

Making a Ten

Children are often comfortable with sums of ten, e.g., $6 + 4 = 10$, and can use them to find differences from ten, e.g., $10 - 6 = 4$ and $10 - 4 = 6$. Students used ten frames to visualize these problems in Grades K–2, as shown in Figure 1. They can then use these facts to find close facts, such as $11 - 4 = 7$.

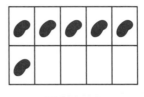

$$10 - 4 = 6$$

Figure 1: *Using a ten frame to visualize $10 - 4 = 6$*

Using a Ten

Students follow the pattern they find when subtracting ten, e.g., $17 - 10 = 7$ and $13 - 10 = 3$, to learn "close facts," e.g., $17 - 9 = 8$ and $13 - 9 = 4$. Since $17 - 9$ will be one more than $17 - 10$, they can reason that the answer will be $7 + 1$ or 8.

Reasoning from Related Addition Facts (Thinking Addition)

To find the answer to $15 - 8$, a student thinks, "8 plus what number equals 15? Since $8 + 7 = 15$, $15 - 8 = 7$."

Resources

- Mathematical Sciences Education Board. *Measuring Up: Prototypes for Mathematics Assessment.* National Academy Press, Washington, DC, 1993.
- National Research Council. "Developing Proficiency with Whole Numbers." In *Adding It Up: Helping Children Learn Mathematics.* J. Kilpatrick, J. Swafford, and B. Findell, eds. National Academy Press, Washington, DC, 2001.
- Payne, J.N. (Ed.). *Mathematics for the Young Child.* The National Council of Teachers of Mathematics, Reston, VA, 1990.
- *Principles and Standards for School Mathematics.* The National Council of Teachers of Mathematics. Reston, VA, 2000.
- Stenmark, J.K. (Ed.). *Mathematics Assessment: Myths, Models, Good Questions, and Practical Suggestions.* The National Council of Teachers of Mathematics, Reston, VA, 1991.
- Thornton, C.A. "Strategies for the Basic Facts." In J.N. Payne (Ed.), *Mathematics for the Young Child.* The National Council of Teachers of Mathematics, Reston, VA, 1990.
- Webb, N.L. (Ed.). *Assessment in the Mathematics Classroom.* The National Council of Teachers of Mathematics, Reston, VA, 1993.

Information for Parents

Grade 3 Math Facts Philosophy

The goal of the math facts strand in *Math Trailblazers* is for students to learn the basic facts efficiently, gain fluency with their use, and retain that fluency over time.

A large body of research supports an approach in which students develop strategies for figuring out the facts rather than relying on rote memorization. This not only leads to more effective learning and better retention, but also to the development of mental math skills. In fact, too much drill before conceptual understanding may interfere with a child's ability to understand concepts at a later date. Therefore, the teaching of the basic facts in *Math Trailblazers* is characterized by the following elements:

Use of Strategies. In all grades we encourage students to use strategies to find facts, so they become confident they can find answers to facts problems they do not immediately recall. In this way, students learn that math is more than memorizing facts and rules which "you either get or you don't."

Distributed Facts Practice. Students study small groups of facts that can be found using similar strategies. In Units 1–10 of third grade, they review the subtraction facts and develop strategies for the multiplication facts. Students focus on developing fluency with the multiplication facts in Units 11–20. They use flash cards at home to study each group of facts.

Practice in Context. Students continue to practice all the facts as they use them to solve problems in the labs, activities, and games.

Appropriate Assessment. Students are regularly assessed to see if they can find answers to facts problems quickly and accurately and retain this skill over time. They take a short quiz on each group of facts. Students record their progress on *Facts I Know* charts and determine which facts they need to study. They take an inventory test of all the subtraction facts at the end of Unit 10 and all the multiplication facts at the end of the year.

A Multiyear Approach. In Grades 1 and 2, the curriculum emphasizes the use of strategies that enable students to develop fluency with the addition and subtraction facts by the end of second grade. In Grade 3, students review the subtraction facts and develop fluency with the multiplication facts. In Grade 4, the addition and subtraction facts are checked, the multiplication facts are reviewed, and students develop fluency with the division facts. In Grade 5, students review the multiplication and division facts.

Facts Will Not Act as Gatekeepers. Use of strategies and calculators allows students to continue to work on interesting problems and experiments while learning the facts. They are not prevented from learning more complex mathematics because they do not have quick recall of the facts.

Información para los padres

El objetivo de la enseñanza de los conceptos matemáticos básicos en *Math Trailblazers* es que los estudiantes aprendan los conceptos básicos eficazmente, logren el dominio del uso de estos conceptos y mantengan ese dominio con el paso del tiempo.

Las extensas investigaciones realizadas respaldan la aplicación de un enfoque en el que los estudiantes desarrollan estrategias para resolver las operaciones en lugar de hacerlo de memoria. Esto no sólo permite un aprendizaje más eficaz y una mejor retención, sino que también promueve el desarrollo de habilidades matemáticas mentales. De hecho, el exceso de repetición antes de comprender los conceptos puede interferir con la habilidad de los niños para entender conceptos más adelante. Por lo tanto, la enseñanza y la evaluación de los conceptos básicos en *Math Trailblazers* se caracteriza por los siguientes elementos:

El uso de estrategias. En todos los grados, alentamos el uso de estrategias para resolver operaciones básicas, de modo que los estudiantes tengan la confianza de que pueden hallar soluciones a problemas que no recuerdan inmediatamente. De esta manera, los estudiantes aprenden que las matemáticas son más que tablas y reglas memorizadas que un estudiante "sabe o no sabe".

Práctica gradual de los conceptos básicos. Los estudiantes estudian pequeños grupos de conceptos básicos que pueden hallarse usando estrategias similares. En las unidades 1 a 10 de tercer grado, repasan las restas básicas y desarrollan estrategias para aprender las tablas de multiplicación. Los estudiantes se concentran en desarrollar el dominio de las tablas de multiplicación en las unidades 11 a 20. Usan tarjetas para estudiar cada grupo pequeño en casa.

Práctica en contexto. Los estudiantes continúan practicando todos los conceptos básicos a medida que los usan para resolver problemas en las investigaciones, las actividades y los juegos.

Evaluación apropiada. Se evalúa con frecuencia a los estudiantes para determinar si pueden hallar la respuesta a problemas relacionados con los conceptos básicos en forma rápida y precisa y si pueden retener esta habilidad con el paso del tiempo. Los estudiantes tomarán una prueba breve sobre cada grupo de conceptos básicos. Los estudiantes registrarán su avance en las tablas tituladas *"Las tablas que conozco"* y determinan qué conceptos básicos necesitan estudiar. Al final de la unidad 10 tomarán una prueba sobre todas las restas básicas y al final del año tomarán una sobre todas las tablas de multiplicación.

Un enfoque que abarca varios años. En primer y segundo grado, el programa da énfasis en el uso de estrategias que permiten a los estudiantes adquirir el dominio de las sumas y restas básicas para fines de segundo grado. En tercer grado, los estudiantes repasan las restas básicas y desarrollan el dominio de las tablas de multiplicación. En cuarto grado, se verifica el aprendizaje de las sumas y restas básicas, se repasan las tablas de multiplicación, y se desarrolla el dominio de las tablas de división. En quinto grado, los estudiantes repasan las tablas de multiplicación y las división.

El nivel de dominio de los conceptos básicos no impedirá el aprendizaje. El uso de estrategias y calculadoras permite a los estudiantes continuar trabajando con problemas y experimentos interesantes mientras aprenden los conceptos básicos. Si los estudiantes no recuerdan fácilmente los conceptos básicos, podrán igualmente aprender conceptos matemáticos más complejos.

Copyright © Kendall/Hunt Publishing Company

Observational Assessment Record

 A1 Can students use strategies to add and subtract?

A2 Can students make and interpret bar graphs?

A3 Can students collect, organize, graph, and analyze data?

A4 Can students use patterns in data tables and graphs to make predictions and solve problems?

A5 Can students communicate mathematical reasoning verbally and in writing?

A6 _____

Name	A1	A2	A3	A4	A5	A6	Comments
1.							
2.							
3.							
4.							
5.							
6.							
7.							
8.							
9.							
10.							
11.							
12.							
13.							

Name	A1	A2	A3	A4	A5	A6	Comments
14.							
15.							
16.							
17.							
18.							
19.							
20.							
21.							
22.							
23.							
24.							
25.							
26.							
27.							
28.							
29.							
30.							
31.							
32.							

Daily Practice and Problems
Strategies: An Assessment Unit

A DPP Menu for Unit 2

Two Daily Practice and Problems (DPP) items are included for each class session listed in the Unit Outline. A scope and sequence chart for the DPP is in the *Teacher Implementation Guide*.

Icons in the Teacher Notes column designate the subject matter of each DPP item. The first item in each class session is always a Bit and the second is either a Task or Challenge. Each item falls into one or more of the categories listed below. A menu of the DPP items for Unit 2 follows.

N Number Sense	✖ Computation	🕐 Time	◇ Geometry
A, C, E, I, K, M, S, W, X	A, B, D, E, M, P, S, W, X	C, D, I	J
$\frac{5}{\times 7}$ Math Facts	$ Money	🎵 Measurement	📈 Data
A, E, L, N, O, Q, R, T, U	B, F–H, V–X		

The Daily Practice and Problems, found at the beginning of each unit, is a set of short exercises that:

- provides distributed practice in computation and a structure for systematic study of the basic math facts;
- develops concepts and skills such as number sense, mental math, telling time, and working with money; and
- reviews topics from earlier units, presenting concepts in new contexts and linking ideas from unit to unit.

There are three types of items: Bits, Tasks, and Challenges. Bits are short and should take no more than five or ten minutes to complete. They usually provide practice with a skill or the basic math facts. Tasks take ten or fifteen minutes to complete. Challenges usually take longer than fifteen minutes to complete and the problems are more thought-provoking. Use them to stretch students'

problem-solving skills. Refer to the Daily *Practice and Problems and Home Practice Guide* in the *Teacher Implementation Guide* for further information on how and when to use the DPP.

Practicing and Assessing Math Facts

By the end of third grade, students are expected to demonstrate fluency with the addition, subtraction, and multiplication facts. In Unit 1 students reviewed and were assessed on the addition facts.

In Unit 2 Lesson 5 students begin the formal review of the subtraction facts through the use of strategies. This review and assessment will continue through Unit 10. Lesson 7 of this unit introduces students to the subtraction facts flash cards and the *Subtraction Facts I Know* chart. Students will use both tools to practice the facts and monitor their own progress. This unit reviews the subtraction facts in Group 1 (12 − 9, 12 − 10, 13 − 9, 13 − 10, 13 − 4, 15 − 9, 15 − 10, 15 − 6, 19 − 10) and Group 2 (14 − 10, 14 − 9, 14 − 5, 17 − 10, 17 − 9, 11 − 9, 16 − 9, 16 − 7, 16 − 10). Facts in these groups can be solved by using a ten. Encourage students to use strategies that make sense to them. See the Background of this unit for a description of efficient strategies for the subtraction facts.

The remaining subtraction facts will be reviewed and assessed in the DPP in Units 3 through 10 according to the schedule in Figure 2. Students will begin studying multiplication in Unit 3. The DPP in the same unit begins a yearlong study of the multiplication facts. See the DPP Guides in Units 3 and 11, the TIMS Tutor: *Math Facts* in the *Teacher Implementation Guide,* and the *Grade 3 Facts Resource Guide* for more information.

Unit	Groups	Focus Facts	Discussion Strategies	Quizzes
2	1 2	12 − 9, 12 − 10, 13 − 9, 13 − 10, 13 − 4, 15 − 9, 15 − 10, 15 − 6, 19 − 10, 14 − 10, 14 − 9, 14 − 5, 17 − 10, 17 − 9, 11 − 9, 16 − 9, 16 − 7, 16 − 10	Using a Ten, Thinking Addition	
3	3 4	10 − 4, 9 − 4, 11 − 4, 10 − 8, 11 − 8, 9 − 5, 10 − 6, 11 − 6, 11 − 5, 10 − 7, 9 − 7, 11 − 7, 10 − 2, 9 − 2, 9 − 3, 10 − 3, 11 − 3, 9 − 6	Making a Ten	
4	5 6	7 − 3, 7 − 5, 7 − 2, 11 − 2, 8 − 6, 5 − 3, 8 − 2, 4 − 2, 5 − 2, 6 − 4, 6 − 2, 13 − 5, 8 − 5, 8 − 3, 13 − 8, 12 − 8, 12 − 4, 12 − 3	Counting Strategies Thinking Addition	
5	7 8	14 − 7, 14 − 6, 14 − 8, 12 − 6, 12 − 7, 12 − 5, 10 − 5, 13 − 7, 13 − 6, 15 − 7, 16 − 8, 17 − 8, 18 − 9, 18 − 10, 8 − 4, 7 − 4, 6 − 3, 15 − 8	Using Doubles	
7	1 & 2		Using a Ten, Thinking Addition	Quiz A
8	3 & 4		Making a Ten	Quiz B
9	5 6		Counting Strategies Thinking Addition	Quiz C
10	7 & 8		Using Doubles	Quiz D Inventory

Figure 2: *Distribution of subtraction facts in Grade 3*

Students may solve the items individually, in groups, or as a class. The items may also be assigned for homework. The DPPs are also available on the Teacher Resource CD.

Student Questions	Teacher Notes

A Quick Addition

Do these problems in your head. Write only the answers.

1. $4 + 9 =$
2. $40 + 90 =$
3. $20 + 90 =$
4. $20 + 30 =$
5. $30 + 50 =$
6. $40 + 60 =$
7. $10 + 90 =$
8. $60 + 80 =$
9. $80 + 70 =$
10. Explain your strategy for Question 9.

TIMS Bit

These problems provide an opportunity for students to review a few addition facts and relate them to adding multiples of ten.

1. 13   2. 130
3. 110   4. 50
5. 80   6. 100
7. 100   8. 140
9. 150

10. Possible strategy: Students may break apart 70 into 20 and 50. Then by joining 20 and 80 to make 100, the remaining 50 is added to equal 150.

B Change

1. You go to the store with $1.00. You buy a pen that costs 73¢. The tax is 6¢. How much change will you get?

2. What coins could you get in change? How many different ways can you answer this question?

TIMS Task

Students may need to use coins to solve these problems.

1. 21¢

2. Possible solutions:

1¢	5¢	10¢
1	0	2
1	2	1
1	4	0
6	1	1
6	3	0
11	2	0
11	0	1
16	1	0
21	0	0

C Calculator Counting

Work with a partner to find how long it will take to count to 100. One partner will count. The other will time how long the counting takes. Take turns.

A. Use a calculator to count by ones to 100. How long did it take?

B. Predict how long it would take to count by twos to 100. Use a calculator to count by twos to 100. How long did it take?

TIMS Bit Ⓝ 🕓

Pressing 1 + = = = on a calculator with an addition constant will cause the calculator to count by ones. To count by twos, press: 2 + = = = = =. Otherwise students can press 2 + 2 + 2 + 2 + 2 + ... or 2 + 2 = + 2 = + 2 = + 2 =. ... You do not necessarily need a calculator to do this activity. However, students will use skip counting on the calculator in later units on multiplication and decimals.

Discuss the results. Did students predict that it would take half as long to count by twos? Were their predictions close? Why or why not?

D Piano Practice

Abbey practices piano every day. Here are the songs she plays and the time it takes to play them:

"Evening Bells"	2 minutes
"Scottish Dance"	1 minute
"Air" by Mozart	$\frac{1}{2}$ minute

A. Can she play all three songs ten times in half an hour?

B. How long will she play if she warms up for five minutes and then plays each song six times?

TIMS Challenge ▨ 🕓

There are many possible strategies for solving these problems. Make sure students explain their solutions.

A. No, since it will take 20 minutes (10 × 2 min) to play "Evening Bells" 10 times and 10 minutes to play the "Scottish Dance" 10 times, it will take her 30 minutes to play them both and she won't have time to play Mozart.

B. 26 minutes. Students may use repeated addition to solve this problem.

Student Questions	Teacher Notes

E Mental Arithmetic: Using Doubles

Solve these problems in your head. Write only the answers. Be ready to explain your answers.

1. 6 + 6 =

2. 6 + 5 =

3. 8 + 6 =

4. 50 + 50 =

5. 60 + 50 =

6. 50 + 55 =

7. 25 + 25 =

8. 25 + 27 =

9. 25 + 15 =

10. Explain your strategy for Question 8.

TIMS Bit

These problems are grouped to encourage students to use doubles to find the answers. For example, 25 + 27 can be solved by doubling 25 and adding two.

(25 + 25 + 2 = 52)

1. 12 2. 11

3. 14 4. 100

5. 110 6. 105

7. 50 8. 52

9. 40

10. Possible strategy: Students may think of adding two quarters to make 50 and then the remaining 2 to make 52.

F Coins

1. Demont needs to pay 80¢. How does he pay if he uses as few coins as possible?

2. Demont needs to pay 70¢. How does he pay if he uses as few coins as possible?

TIMS Task $

Students may need coins to solve these problems.

1. 3 quarters and 1 nickel

2. 2 quarters and 2 dimes

G Money Problems

Hugo pays 72¢ for a Super Ball. He gives the sales clerk one dollar.

A. How much change will Hugo get?

B. What coins might the cashier give him?

TIMS Bit $

Students may need coins to solve these problems. Hugo will receive 28¢ in change. There are many solutions for the second part. He might receive a quarter and three pennies or two dimes, one nickel, and three pennies.

More Coins

List all the ways to make 15¢.

TIMS Challenge

Students may need coins to solve these problems.

1¢	5¢	10¢
0	3	0
5	2	0
0	1	1
10	1	0
15	0	0
5	0	1

I **More Calculator Counting**

Take turns counting and timing with a partner.

A. Predict how long it will take to count by fives to 100. Use a calculator to count by fives to 100. How long did it take?

B. Predict how long it will take to count by tens to 100. Use a calculator to count by tens to 100. How long did it take?

TIMS Bit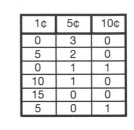

See Bit C for information on skip counting on the calculator. Discuss the results. How did students make their predictions? Did students use the results of C to help make their predictions? Were the predictions reasonable? Were the predictions close to the actual time? Why or why not?

One way to investigate the questions is to make a frequency distribution of all students' times for counting by fives and then by tens. What time occurred most often? Do the other times cluster around this bar?

J **Square Corners**

Look around the classroom for corners that are "square." You can check to see if they are really square by comparing the corners to the corner of your paper.

A. Make a list of square-cornered objects.

B. Make a list of corners that are not square.

TIMS Task

You may wish to keep a list of square-cornered objects and a list of corners that are not square. Students can continue to add new items to the list.

Student Questions	Teacher Notes

K Pencils in the Classroom

Estimate the number of pencils in your classroom right now. Explain how you made your estimate.

TIMS Bit   [N]

Students might count the number of pencils in several different desks and estimate an average number of pencils per desk. Then they might use a calculator to multiply or use repeated addition to find an answer for all the desks in the class. Since many strategies are possible, the class can compare and contrast different methods. Emphasize the fact that an exact answer is not needed.

L Line Math Puzzle

Put the digits 4, 5, 6, 7, and 8 in the boxes so that the sum of each line is the same.

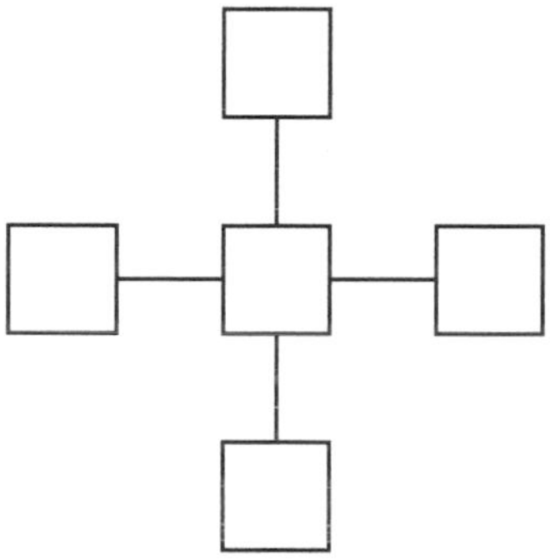

TIMS Task   [×⁵⁷]

One possible solution:

```
        5
        |
  4 --- 6 --- 8
        |
        7
```

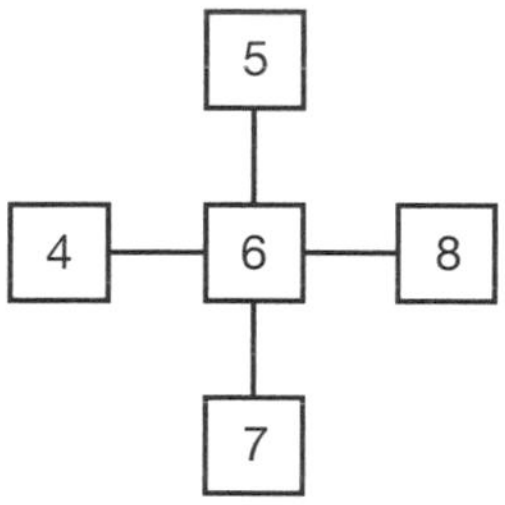

M 1 and 0 Are Broken

The "1" key and the "0" key are broken on the calculator. List the keys you would press to do these problems.

A. 10 + 10

B. 11 + 10

C. 11 + 11

TIMS Bit   [N] [✖]

Students should compare solutions. Some may need to check their work on a calculator.

Student Questions	Teacher Notes

(N) Magic Square: 4, 5, 6

Complete the magic square using the digits 4, 4, 4, 5, 5, 5, 6, 6, and 6. Each row, column, and diagonal must have a sum of 15.

<table>
<tr><td></td><td></td><td></td></tr>
<tr><td></td><td></td><td></td></tr>
<tr><td></td><td></td><td></td></tr>
</table>

TIMS Task $\boxed{\times \frac{5}{7}}$

Students may write the digits on slips of paper and use them to fill in the magic square. If students have difficulty, suggest that they put a five in the middle. One solution:

4	6	5
6	5	4
5	4	6

Ask students to compare this magic square to those in the *Magic Squares* activity. How are they alike? How are they different?

(O) Some Sums

Alex wrote the following number sentences to show six and seven broken into two parts.

$3 + 3 = 6$ $6 + 1 = 7$

Write other number sentences to show six and seven broken into two parts.

TIMS Bit $\boxed{\times \frac{5}{7}}$

Other number sentences include:

$0 + 6 = 6$	$0 + 7 = 7$
$6 + 0 = 6$	$7 + 0 = 7$
$1 + 5 = 6$	$1 + 6 = 7$
$5 + 1 = 6$	$2 + 5 = 7$
$2 + 4 = 6$	$5 + 2 = 7$
$4 + 2 = 6$	$3 + 4 = 7$
	$4 + 3 = 7$

(P) Number Sentence Stories

Write a story for the following number sentence.

$25 = 19 +$ _____

TIMS Task ⊠

Students may write:
"There are twenty-five students in our class. Nineteen students are wearing sneakers. Six students are wearing boots."

Student Questions	Teacher Notes

Q What's Your Strategy?

Bill has trouble remembering the answer to 15 − 8. What strategy might be helpful for Bill?

TIMS Bit

Bill might use ten:

from 8 to 10 is 2

from 10 to 15 is 5

So 15 − 8 = 7

or

15 − 5 = 10

10 − 3 = 7

R Magic Square Mystery

Complete the magic square using the numbers 5, 6, 7, 10, and 11. Each row, column, and diagonal must have the same sum. What is the sum?

9	4	
	8	
	12	

TIMS Challenge

9	4	11
10	8	6
5	12	7

The sum is 24. Once students have found the solution, ask them to look at the magic square and look for patterns. Where are the odd and even numbers? (All of the odd numbers are on the corners.)

S 1 and 2 Are Broken

The "1" key and the "2" key are broken on the calculator. List the keys you would press to do these problems.

A. 12 + 12

B. 12 + 11

C. 20 + 20

TIMS Bit

Students should compare solutions. Some may need to check their work on a calculator.

T **Magic Square: Sum = 15**

Complete the magic square using 1, 2, 3, 4, 5, 6, 7, 8, and 9. Each row, column, and diagonal must have a sum of 15. This is the same magic square that Sun Feng had to do in the story *Yü the Great*.

TIMS Challenge

4	9	2
3	5	7
8	1	6

The solution above can also be found in the design on the turtle's back in the story *Yü the Great*. There are many solutions, but each solution has 5 in the center square. Challenge students to find more solutions. If students have difficulty, suggest that they put 5 in the middle.

U **Addition Sentences**

Write two addition sentences for each of the following sums.

A. 13

B. 17

C. 10

D. 11

TIMS Bit

Students should compare solutions. Students may use different addends and a different number of addends. Some may need to check their work on a calculator.

V **More Coins**

List all the ways to make 40¢ without using pennies.

TIMS Challenge

Students may use coins to solve this problem.

5¢	10¢	25¢
8	0	0
6	1	0
4	2	0
3	0	1
2	3	0
1	1	1
0	4	0

Fruit for $2

These are the fruit prices at Fred's Fantastic Fruit Farm. You have $2 to spend.

Apples   33¢ each

Apple Cider   75¢ per quart

Pears   50¢ each

Grapes   65¢ a bunch

Plums   24¢ each

1. Can you buy four pears?
   Why or why not?

2. Can you buy eight plums?
   Why or why not?

3. Can you buy four bunches of grapes?
   Why or why not?

TIMS Bit

Discuss student methods for finding a solution.

Ask similar questions using the prices of other fruits.

1. Yes, 50¢ + 50¢ + 50¢ + 50¢ = $2

2. Yes, 24¢ is less than 25¢. 8 quarters make $2.

3. No, 65¢ is greater than 50¢.

X **More Fruit for $2**

These are the fruit prices at Fred's Fantastic Fruit Farm. You have $2 to spend.

Apples   33¢ each

Apple Cider   75¢ per quart

Pears   50¢ each

Grapes   65¢ a bunch

Plums   24¢ each

Figure out these problems in your head:

A. Can you buy an apple, one bunch of grapes, and a quart of apple cider?

B. What would you buy for $2?

TIMS Task

One strategy for solving the first problem is to think in terms such as "more than half a dollar" or "less than half a dollar." For example, since grapes are 15¢ more than 50¢ and apple cider is about 30¢ more than 50¢, then the grapes and apple cider together are about 50¢ + 15¢ + 30¢ + 50¢ or $1.45. Since 33¢ is less than a half dollar, there is still enough money to buy the apple, too. Encourage students to share their strategies in class discussion.

Lesson 1

Addition Facts Strategies

Lesson Overview

Students review addition strategies and use them to solve problems with more than two addends.

Key Content

- Using strategies to add.
- Using turn-around facts (commutativity) to add.
- Using grouping strategies (associativity) to add.
- Developing calculator skills.
- Developing mental math skills.

Key Vocabulary

- addend
- keystrokes
- sum

Math Facts

DPP Bit A provides practice with math facts.

Homework

1. Assign the *Switch It!* Homework Page in the *Discovery Assignment Book.*
2. Assign the *Calculator Explorations* Homework Page.

Assessment

Students complete the *Calculator Challenges* Assessment Page.

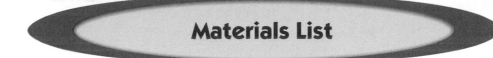

Materials List

Supplies and Copies

Student	Teacher
Supplies for Each Student Pair • 40 connecting cubes • calculator	**Supplies**

Copies
 	
• 1 copy of *Calculator Challenges* per student
  (*Unit Resource Guide* Page 36)
	Copies/Transparencies
	
	• 1 transparency of *Calculator Explorations,* optional
	  (*Discovery Assignment Book* Page 27)

All blackline masters including assessment, transparency, and DPP masters are also on the Teacher Resource CD.

Student Books

Addition Facts Strategies (*Student Guide* Pages 14–15)
Switch It! (*Discovery Assignment Book* Page 25)
Calculator Explorations (*Discovery Assignment Book* Page 27)

Daily Practice and Problems and Home Practice

DPP items A–D (*Unit Resource Guide* Pages 19–20)

Note: Classrooms whose pacing differs significantly from the suggested pacing of the units should use the Math Facts Calendar in Section 4 of the *Facts Resource Guide* to ensure students receive the complete math facts program.

Daily Practice and Problems

Suggestions for using the DPPs are on page 34.

A. Bit: Quick Addition (URG p. 19)

Do these problems in your head. Write only the answers.

1. $4 + 9 =$
2. $40 + 90 =$
3. $20 + 90 =$
4. $20 + 30 =$
5. $30 + 50 =$
6. $40 + 60 =$
7. $10 + 90 =$
8. $60 + 80 =$
9. $80 + 70 =$
10. Explain your strategy for Question 9.

B. Task: Change (URG p. 19)

1. You go to the store with $1.00. You buy a pen that costs 73¢. The tax is 6¢. How much change will you get?
2. What coins could you get in change? How many different ways can you answer this question?

C. Bit: Calculator Counting (URG p. 20)

Work with a partner to find how long it will take to count to 100. One partner will count. The other will time how long the counting takes. Take turns.

A. Use a calculator to count by ones to 100. How long did it take?

B. Predict how long it would take to count by twos to 100. Use a calculator to count by twos to 100. How long did it take?

D. Challenge: Piano Practice
(URG p. 20)

Abbey practices piano every day. Here are the songs she plays and the time it takes to play them:

"Evening Bells"   2 minutes

"Scottish Dance"   1 minute

"Air" by Mozart $\frac{1}{2}$ minute

A. Can she play each song ten times in half an hour?

B. How long will she play if she warms up for five minutes and then plays each song six times?

Part 1 Using a Ten

Give each pair forty connecting cubes. Ask students to build a train with seven blue cubes and another train with eight red cubes. Ask:

- *What can you do with the cubes to make a train of ten?* (Move two blue cubes to the train of eight or move three red cubes to the train of seven.)

- *You now have a train of ten cubes and a train of five cubes. What is the sum?* (15)

- *Why is this problem (10 + 5) easier to solve than the first one (7 + 8)?*

Ask students to repeat this procedure and find groups of ten to do problems such as 6 + 7, 8 + 8, and 8 + 9.

Discuss how using a ten can help students remember some addition facts.

Part 2 Switch It!

Ask students to solve 14 + 7 + 6 with connecting cubes. They can use a different color to represent each addend. Ask students to group the cubes in as many tens as possible to achieve the sum. One way to find the sum:

- Break apart the fourteen into ten and four;

- Group the six cubes with the four cubes to make a ten;

- Represent the sum with two trains of ten cubes and a train of seven cubes.

Ask students to share their methods. Challenge them to complete 14 + 7 + 6 using mental arithmetic. It is easier to solve if the addends are first rearranged to find groups or multiples of ten. (14 + 6 = 20, then 20 + 7 = 27)

Give students other problems:

- 8 + 7 + 12

- 6 + 8 + 14

- 11 + 3 + 9

Encourage them to find groups of tens with the cubes and then do the arithmetic mentally. Note that other strategies can be equally efficient. For example, students may choose to use doubles to add 6 + 8 + 14 = 14 + 14 = 28.

Students should then read the dialog on the *Addition Facts Strategies* Activity Pages and do the Switching problems. Ask students to explain how they did the problems. Assign the *Switch It!* Homework Page.

Student Guide - page 14

Content Note

The concepts introduced in this unit are formally known as the commutative and associative properties of addition. The **commutative property,** sometimes called the order property, means that when adding a series of numbers, the order in which they are added makes no difference. For example, when adding 5 + 6 + 5 the same answer is reached whether the numbers are added in the order given or not (5 + 6 + 5 = 5 + 5 + 6).

The **associative property** means that numbers may be grouped in different configurations when adding. An example is 4 + 8 + 2. The numbers may be added by grouping the 4 + 8 first and then adding the 2:

(4 + 8) + 2 = 12 + 2 = 14. In the alternative, the 8 + 2 can be grouped before the 4 is added:

4 + (8 + 2) = 4 + 10 = 14.

Students need not know the formal names for these properties, but they should develop the ability to use them when adding.

Part 3

Breaking Addends into Parts

Sometimes addends can be easily grouped into tens; however, this may not always be obvious. A worthwhile strategy for adding mentally is partitioning addends before finding groups of ten. For example, in the problem here the second addend, 5, can be rewritten as $3 + 2$.

$$7 + \mathbf{5} + 2$$

$$7 + \mathbf{3} + \mathbf{2} + 2$$

Students can now group $7 + 3$, and find the sum $10 + 2 + 2 = 14$.

Give students similar problems to solve:

- $6 + 8 + 3$
- $9 + 7 + 2$
- $4 + 9 + 3$

Students should discuss and compare solutions.

As students become adept at partitioning single-digit numbers, introduce two-digit addends in problems such as $11 + 5 + 3$; $2 + 19 + 5$; and $12 + 9 + 15$. Ask students to explain how they did the problems. As students share their solutions, ask:

- *Did anyone find another way to solve that problem?*

Ask students to complete the problems in the Breaking Addends into Parts section in the *Student Guide*.

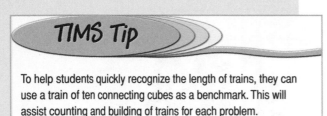

To help students quickly recognize the length of trains, they can use a train of ten connecting cubes as a benchmark. This will assist counting and building of trains for each problem.

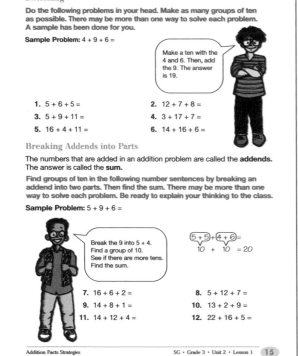

Switching

Do the following problems in your head. Make as many groups of ten as possible. There may be more than one way to solve each problem. A sample has been done for you.

Sample Problem: $4 + 9 + 6 =$

Make a ten with the 4 and 6. Then, add the 9. The answer is 19.

1. $5 + 6 + 5 =$
2. $12 + 7 + 8 =$
3. $5 + 9 + 11 =$
4. $3 + 17 + 7 =$
5. $16 + 4 + 11 =$
6. $14 + 16 + 6 =$

Breaking Addends into Parts

The numbers that are added in an addition problem are called the **addends.** The answer is called the **sum.**

Find groups of ten in the following number sentences by breaking an addend into two parts. Then find the sum. There may be more than one way to solve each problem. Be ready to explain your thinking to the class.

Sample Problem: $5 + 9 + 6 =$

Break the 9 into $5 + 4$. Find a group of 10. See if there are more tens. Find the sum.

$\underbrace{5 + 5} + \underbrace{4 + 6} =$
$10 + 10 = 20$

7. $16 + 6 + 2 =$
8. $5 + 12 + 7 =$
9. $14 + 8 + 1 =$
10. $13 + 2 + 9 =$
11. $14 + 12 + 4 =$
12. $22 + 16 + 5 =$

Addition Facts Strategies   SG • Grade 3 • Unit 2 • Lesson 1   15

***Student Guide* - page 15** *(Answers on p. 37)*

Part 4 My Calculator Is Broken!

In this part, students partition addends using calculators. Begin by saying:

- *Today, we are going to imagine that some of the keys on the calculator are broken. That means that you cannot use those keys. First, let's imagine the five is broken. What keys would you press to do the problem 9 + 5 + 2?*

There are a number of ways to key this problem without using the five key. Encourage students to partition five so that a group of ten can be formed. For example, students might enter the following keystrokes:

Some students might skip a step on the calculator and press:

Provide additional problems that include addends such as 5, 15, or 25. For example:

- 8 + 5
- 5 + 7 + 6
- 15 + 6 + 3
- 9 + 25

Encourage students to predict the calculator's answer before they key it into the calculator. Ask students to list their keystrokes on the board or overhead. Encourage students to compare different keystroke sequences.

Assign the *Calculator Explorations* Homework Page.

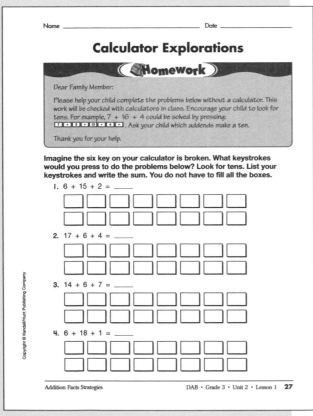

Math Facts

DPP Bit A provides practice with math facts and
adding numbers with ending zeros.

Homework and Practice

- Students switch the order of addends to make
groups of ten on the *Switch It!* Homework Page
in the *Discovery Assignment Book.*

- On the *Calculator Explorations* Homework Page
in the *Discovery Assignment Book,* the six key is
broken. Students complete this page at home
without using a calculator and then check their
work in class. You may want to make a transparency and model an example.

- DPP Task B provides practice with money and
calculating change. Bit C develops number sense
through skip counting on a calculator. For
Challenge D, students make calculations involving elapsed time.

Assessment

Use the *Calculator Challenges* Assessment
Blackline Master to measure students' abilities to
partition and rearrange addends.

Extension

Challenge students to group three or more addends
to make a group of ten. For example:

- $3 + 4 + 5 + 3$
- $2 + 5 + 6 + 2 + 1$
- $17 + 5 + 2 + 1$

At a Glance

Math Facts and Daily Practice and Problems

DPP Bit A provides practice with math facts. Task B provides practice with money. Bit C is skip counting on a calculator. Challenge D involves elapsed time.

Part 1. Using a Ten

1. Students build a train with seven blue cubes and another train with eight red cubes.
2. Review the using-ten strategy and have students model it with their cubes.
3. Students utilize the using-ten strategy and their cubes to solve more problems.
4. Students discuss how using a ten can help them add.

Part 2. Switch It!

1. Students solve 14 + 7 + 6 with connecting cubes and share their methods with the class.
2. Students complete 14 + 7 + 6 using mental arithmetic.
3. Students solve other problems: 8 + 7 + 12, 6 + 8 + 14, and 11 + 3 + 9.
4. Students read the *Addition Facts Strategies* Activity Pages in the *Student Guide* and do the problems in the Switching section.
5. Students discuss various solutions.

Part 3. Breaking Addends into Parts

1. Students partition addends to find groups of ten. They discuss and compare solutions.
2. Students solve two-digit addends in problems such as 11 + 5 + 3 and discuss their solutions.
3. Students complete the problems in the Breaking Addends into Parts section in the *Student Guide.*

Part 4. My Calculator Is Broken!

1. Students discuss how they might solve a problem on an imaginary calculator with a broken five key.
2. Students partition five so that a group of ten can be formed.
3. Students work additional problems that include addends such as 5, 15, or 25. Students list their keystrokes on the board or overhead.
4. Students practice predicting the calculator's answer before they key it into the calculator.
5. Students compare different keystroke sequences.

Homework

1. Assign the *Switch It!* Homework Page in the *Discovery Assignment Book.*
2. Assign the *Calculator Explorations* Homework Page.

Assessment

Students complete the *Calculator Challenges* Assessment Page.

Extension

Have students group three or four addends to make ten.

Answer Key is on pages 37–38.

Notes:

Calculator Challenges

Imagine the 7 key on your calculator is broken. What keys would you press to do the problems below? Look for tens. List your keystrokes and write the sum. You do not have to fill all the boxes.

1.   7 + 14 + 2 = _____

☐ ☐ ☐ ☐ ☐ ☐ ☐ ☐
☐ ☐ ☐ ☐ ☐ ☐ ☐ ☐

2.   15 + 7 + 4 = _____

☐ ☐ ☐ ☐ ☐ ☐ ☐ ☐
☐ ☐ ☐ ☐ ☐ ☐ ☐ ☐

3.   13 + 6 + 7 = _____

☐ ☐ ☐ ☐ ☐ ☐ ☐ ☐
☐ ☐ ☐ ☐ ☐ ☐ ☐ ☐

4.   7 + 18 + 1 = _____

☐ ☐ ☐ ☐ ☐ ☐ ☐ ☐
☐ ☐ ☐ ☐ ☐ ☐ ☐ ☐

5.   9 + 17 + 4 = _____

☐ ☐ ☐ ☐ ☐ ☐ ☐ ☐
☐ ☐ ☐ ☐ ☐ ☐ ☐ ☐

Assessment Blackline Master

Student Guide (p. 15)

Solution strategies may vary.

1. $16; 5 + 5 = 10; 10 + 6 = 16$
2. $27; 12 + 8 = 20; 20 + 7 = 27$
3. $25; 9 + 11 = 20; 20 + 5 = 25$
4. $27; 3 + 17 = 20; 20 + 7 = 27$
5. $31; 16 + 4 = 20; 20 + 10 + 1 = 31$
6. $36; 14 + 6 = 20; 20 + 16 = 36$
7. $24;$ break the 6 into $4 + 2; 16 + 4 = 20;$
   $20 + 2 + 2 = 24$
8. $24;$ break the 5 into $2 + 3; 3 + 7 = 10;$
   $10 + 12 + 2 = 24$
9. $23;$ break the 8 into $6 + 2; 14 + 6 = 20;$
   $20 + 2 + 1 = 23$
10. $24;$ break the 2 into $1 + 1; 9 + 1 = 10;$
    $10 + 1 + 13 = 24$
11. $30;$ break the 12 into $6 + 6; 14 + 6 = 20$
    and $6 + 4 = 10; 10 + 20 = 30$
12. $43;$ break the 5 into $4 + 1; 16 + 4 = 20;$
    $20 + 22 + 1 = 43$

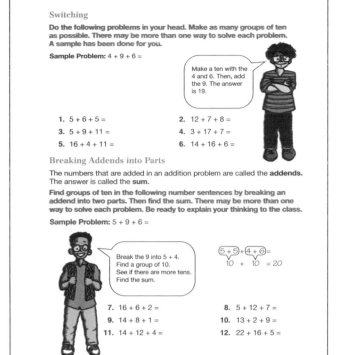

Student Guide - page 15

Discovery Assignment Book (p. 25)

Switch It!

Solution strategies will vary.

1. A. $26; 3 + 7 + 16 = 26$
   B. $27; 9 + 1 + 17 = 27$
   C. $21; 8 + 2 + 11 = 21$
   D. $26; 5 + 5 + 10 + 6 = 26$
   E. $27; 12 + 8 + 7 = 27$
2. Problems will vary.

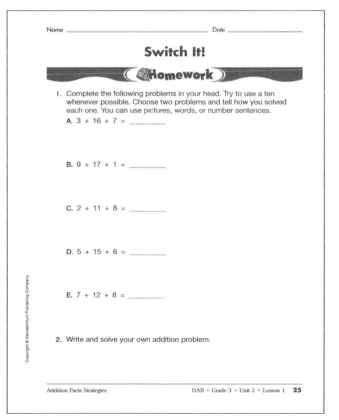

Discovery Assignment Book - page 25

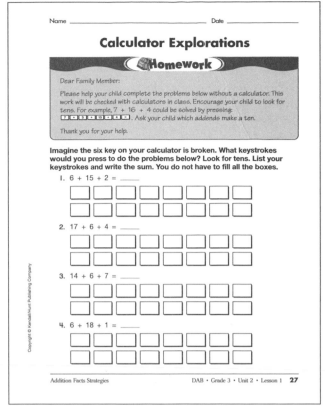

Discovery Assignment Book - page 27

Discovery Assignment Book (p. 27)

Calculator Explorations

Solution strategies/keystrokes will vary.

  1.   23; $1 + 5 + 15 + 2 =$

  2.   27; $17 + 3 + 3 + 4 =$

  3.   27; $14 + 3 + 3 + 7 =$

  4.   25; $4 + 2 + 18 + 1 =$

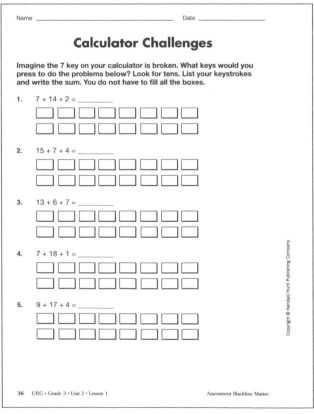

Unit Resource Guide - page 36

Unit Resource Guide (p. 36)

Calculator Challenges

Solution strategies/keystrokes will vary.

  1.   23; $1 + 6 + 14 + 2 =$

  2.   26; $15 + 5 + 2 + 4 =$

  3.   26; $13 + 6 + 4 + 3 =$

  4.   26; $5 + 2 + 18 + 1 =$

  5.   30; $9 + 1 + 16 + 4 =$

Lesson 2

Spinning Sums

Lesson Overview

Estimated Class Sessions
2

This activity provides an opportunity for students to review the addition facts while conducting an investigation. Students spin two spinners to randomly generate addition fact problems. They record these facts in a data table and graph the number of times they spin each sum.

Key Content

- Reviewing the addition facts.
- Using patterns in data to make predictions and solve problems.
- Using turn-around facts (commutativity) to add.

Key Vocabulary

- least common
- most common
- sum
- turn-around facts

Math Facts

DPP Bit E provides practice with math facts. Parts 1 and 2 of the Home Practice provide addition and subtraction practice.

Homework

Assign Home Practice Parts 1 and 2.

Assessment

Use the *Observational Assessment Record* to note students' abilities to use strategies to add quickly and accurately.

Materials List

Supplies and Copies

Student	Teacher
Supplies for Each Student Group • clear plastic spinner (or pencils with paper clips)	**Supplies** • blank transparency, optional
Copies • 1 copy of *Horizontal Bar Graph* per student group (*Unit Resource Guide* Page 50)	**Copies/Transparencies** • 1 transparency of *Spinners 2–9* (*Discovery Assignment Book* Page 29) • 1 transparency of *Spinning Sums Data Table* (*Discovery Assignment Book* Page 31) • 1 transparency of *Horizontal Bar Graph* (*Unit Resource Guide* Page 50) • 1 copy of *Observational Assessment Record* to be used throughout this unit (*Unit Resource Guide* Pages 15–16)

All blackline masters including assessment, transparency, and DPP masters are also on the Teacher Resource CD.

Student Books
Spinning Sums (*Student Guide* Pages 16–18)
Spinners 2–9 (*Discovery Assignment Book* Page 29)
Spinning Sums Data Table (*Discovery Assignment Book* Page 31)

Daily Practice and Problems and Home Practice
DPP items E–H (*Unit Resource Guide* Pages 21–22)
Home Practice Parts 1–2 (*Discovery Assignment Book* Page 22)

Note: Classrooms whose pacing differs significantly from the suggested pacing of the units should use the Math Facts Calendar in Section 4 of the *Facts Resource Guide* to ensure students receive the complete math facts program.

Assessment Tools
Observational Assessment Record (*Unit Resource Guide* Pages 15–16)

Daily Practice and Problems

Suggestions for using the DPPs are on page 48.

E. Bit: Mental Arithmetic: Using Doubles (URG p. 21)

$\boxed{\text{N}}$ $\boxed{\text{×}}$ $\boxed{\frac{5}{\times 7}}$

Solve these problems in your head. Write only the answers. Be ready to explain your answers.

1. $6 + 6 =$
2. $6 + 5 =$
3. $8 + 6 =$
4. $50 + 50 =$
5. $60 + 50 =$
6. $50 + 55 =$
7. $25 + 25 =$
8. $25 + 27 =$
9. $25 + 15 =$
10. Explain your strategy for Question 8.

F. Task: Coins (URG p. 21)

$\boxed{\$}$

1. Demont needs to pay 80¢. How does he pay if he uses as few coins as possible?
2. Demont needs to pay 70¢. How does he pay if he uses as few coins as possible?

G. Bit: Money Problems (URG p. 21)

$\boxed{\$}$

Hugo pays 72¢ for a Super Ball. He gives the sales clerk one dollar.

A. How much change will Hugo get?
B. What coins might the cashier give him?

H. Challenge: More Coins (URG p. 22)

$\boxed{\$}$

List all the ways to make 15¢.

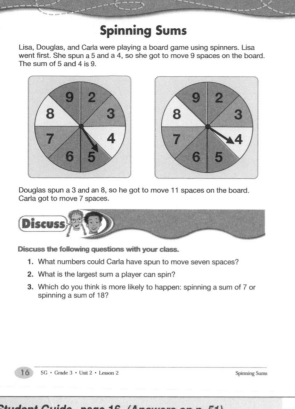

Spinning Sums

Lisa, Douglas, and Carla were playing a board game using spinners. Lisa went first. She spun a 5 and a 4, so she got to move 9 spaces on the board. The sum of 5 and 4 is 9.

Douglas spun a 3 and an 8, so he got to move 11 spaces on the board. Carla got to move 7 spaces.

Discuss

Discuss the following questions with your class.

1. What numbers could Carla have spun to move seven spaces?
2. What is the largest sum a player can spin?
3. Which do you think is more likely to happen: spinning a sum of 7 or spinning a sum of 18?

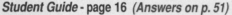

Student Guide - page 16 (Answers on p. 51)

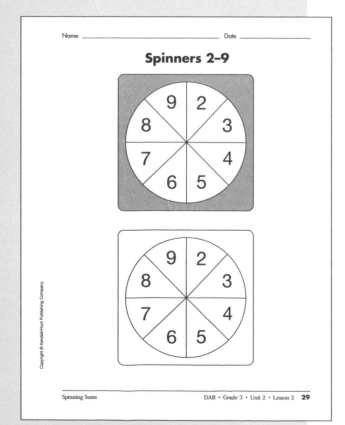

Name _____ Date _____

Spinners 2–9

Spinning Sums   DAB • Grade 3 • Unit 2 • Lesson 2 **29**

Discovery Assignment Book - page 29

Before the Activity

To collect the data, each group of three students can use two clear plastic spinners to cover the white and gray spinners on *Spinners 2–9* in the *Discovery Assignment Book*. If you do not have clear spinners, you can use pencils and paper clips. Straighten out one end of the paper clip, and place a pencil through the curved end. Then, put the point of the pencil on the center of the circle, and spin the paper clip around the pencil, using the straightened end as a pointer.

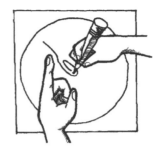

Figure 3: *Using a pencil and paper clip as a spinner*

Teaching the Activity

Show students the two spinners on *Spinners 2–9*. They will use these spinners to create number sentences. Ask the class to decide which spinner they will use for the first number in the number sentences and which for the second. This relationship should remain the same throughout this investigation. Spin both spinners, and write down the resulting number sentence. Remind students that a **sum** is the answer to an addition problem. Read and discuss *Spinning Sums* in the *Student Guide*.

Content Note

The facts $3 + 2 = 5$ and $2 + 3 = 5$ are sometimes called **turn-around facts**, i.e., facts that are identical except for the order of the addends. Remind students that the order of the numbers in an addition number sentence will not change the sum. (See the Content Note on the commutative property in Lesson 1.) In this investigation, however, we will consider $3 + 2 = 5$ and $2 + 3 = 5$ as two different number sentences. We do this because we need to count all possible ways to spin each sum accurately to find the most common sum. Theoretically, a sum of 5 will occur twice as often as a sum of 4 because there are two ways to spin a 5 ($3 + 2$ and $2 + 3$) and only one way to spin a 4 ($2 + 2$).

Since players can spin more than one number sentence for a sum of seven, **Question 1** has more than one answer. Write down all the possible number sentences for Carla's spins: $5 + 2 = 7$, $2 + 5 = 7$, $3 + 4 = 7$, and $4 + 3 = 7$. **Question 3** provides an opportunity to discuss why one sum might occur more often than another. Discuss how the class can answer the question. Guide them to the idea of spinning the spinners and recording the sums.

At this point, introduce the *Spinning Sums Data Table*. To fill in the column labeled "Sum," discuss with students what sums are possible using these spinners.

* *What is the smallest sum possible?* (Since 2 is the smallest number on each spinner, the smallest sum is 4.)

* *What is the largest possible sum?* (Since 9 is the largest number on each spinner, the largest sum is 18.) With this information, students can fill in the Sum column with the numbers 4 through 18.

Collecting Group Data

You can model the data collection procedure on a transparency of *Spinning Sums Data Table* with the help of two students. The students will spin the two spinners at the same time. To record the spin, write down the number sentence in the middle column of the row that reflects its sum. When students understand the procedure, they can begin working in groups to collect data. Groups of three students—two students spinning and the third recording the number sentence—work well for this activity. It is important that students record each spin even if they have already recorded the number sentences. Record number sentences for 40 spins.

The data reflected in the graph in the *Student Guide* is shown in Figure 4. Note that students recorded the number sentence $3 + 6 = 9$ three times since they spun it three times. Students then display the data in a graph, as shown in the *Student Guide*. **Questions 4–10** help students discover, through discussion, the connection between the shape of the graph and the most common and least common sums.

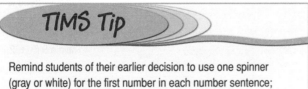

TIMS Tip

Remind students of their earlier decision to use one spinner (gray or white) for the first number in each number sentence; it is important to follow this convention consistently.

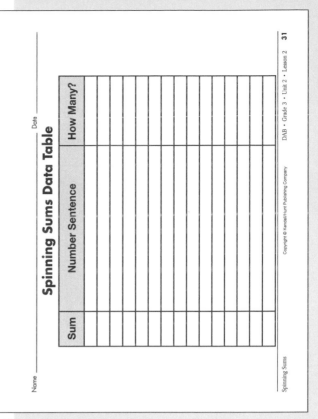

Discovery Assignment Book - page 31 *(Answers on p. 53)*

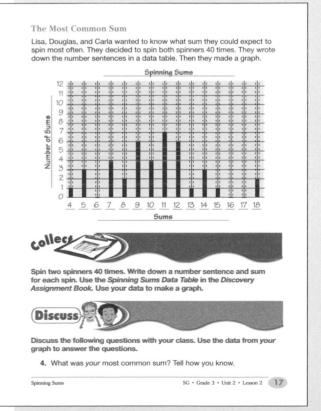

The Most Common Sum

Lisa, Douglas, and Carla wanted to know what sum they could expect to spin most often. They decided to spin both spinners 40 times. They wrote down the number sentences in a data table. Then they made a graph.

Spin two spinners 40 times. Write down a number sentence and sum for each spin. Use the *Spinning Sums Data Table* in the *Discovery Assignment Book*. Use your data to make a graph.

Discuss the following questions with your class. Use the data from *your* graph to answer the questions.

4. What was *your* most common sum? Tell how you know.

Spinning Sums   SG • Grade 3 • Unit 2 • Lesson 2   17

Student Guide - page 17 *(Answers on p. 51)*

Spinning Sums

Sum	Number Sentence	How Many?
4	2 + 2 = 4	1
5	2 + 3 = 5, 3 + 2 = 5, 3 + 2 = 5	3
6		0
7	4 + 3 = 7, 4 + 3 = 7, 5 + 2 = 7, 2 + 5 = 7	4
8	2 + 6 = 8, 6 + 2 = 8	2
9	3 + 6 = 9, 3 + 6 = 9, 3 + 6 = 9, 7 + 2 = 9, 4 + 5 = 9, 2 + 7 = 9	6
10	2 + 8 = 10, 8 + 2 = 10, 7 + 3 = 10, 8 + 2 = 10	4
11	2 + 9 = 11, 4 + 7 = 11, 3 + 8 = 11, 2 + 9 = 11, 4 + 7 = 11, 2 + 9 = 11, 6 + 5 = 11	7
12	4 + 8 = 12, 8 + 4 = 12, 5 + 7 = 12, 9 + 3 = 12, 5 + 7 = 12, 6 + 6 = 12	6
13	4 + 9 = 13	1
14	9 + 5 = 14, 5 + 9 = 14, 7 + 7 = 14	3
15	6 + 9 = 15	1
16		0
17		0
18	9 + 9 = 18, 9 + 9 = 18	2

Figure 4: *A sample student data table*

5. What is *your* least common sum? Tell how you know.

6. Where are the tallest bars on your graph? What does it mean when the bars are tall?

7. Where are the shortest bars on your graph? What does it mean when the bars are short?

8. The graph Lisa, Douglas, and Carla made has taller bars in the middle. How does your graph compare?

9. Compare your graph to the other graphs in the class. How are they the same? How are they different?

10. Are the most common sums in the same place on all the graphs? What about the least common sums?

11. Write a paragraph comparing your graph to the class chart. Make sure you answer these questions:
   • How are your graph and the class chart alike or different?
   • Are the highest points on your graph and the class chart in the same place? What do they tell you?
   • Are the lowest points on your graph and the class chart in the same place? What do they tell you?

As a class, make a chart with all of the possible spins and sums.

 18 SG • Grade 3 • Unit 2 • Lesson 2   Spinning Sums

Student Guide - page 18 (Answers on p. 52)

Creating a Chart from Class Data

Compare the results all of the groups. Did they get similar results? The highest bars will probably be near the middle of most of the graphs because the most common sums (10, 11, and 12) are in the middle of the graph. The shortest bars will probably be at either end since the least common sums (4, 5, 17, and 18) are at the ends of the graph. Why are the most common and least common sums clustered like this? To answer this question, you will create a number sentence chart, which will eventually look like the one in Figure 5.

To build the chart, you will need to write the sums 4 through 18 along the bottom of the board or a transparency. Ask students to look for all the possible number sentences for each sum. As students say each number sentence, write it down above the appropriate sum. The following tables show you how a teacher guided students in creating their number sentence chart.

> **TIMS Tip**
>
> Have students save their copies of *Spinners 2–9* for reuse in the *Spinning Differences* Assessment Activity.

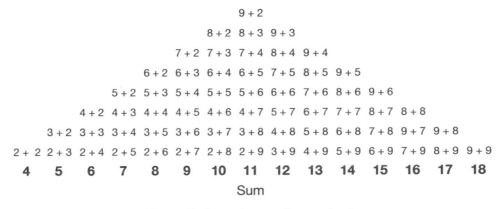

Figure 5: *A number sentence chart for the sums 4 through 18*

Creating a Number Sentence Chart for Sums 4 through 8

Teacher Prompt	Student Response	Teacher Response
Did any group spin two numbers whose sum is 4?	Yes, we got 2 + 2 = 4.	Writes 2 + 2 above 4.
Did anyone get 4 a different way?	No.	
Why do you think no one got 4 a different way?	Because there are no other numbers on the spinner that make a sum of 4	
Did anyone get two numbers that add up to 5?	We did. We got 3 + 2.	Writes 3 + 2 above 5 and says, "All groups who got 3 + 2 = 5 circle 3 + 2 = 5 on your data table."
Are there any other ways to get a sum of 5?	We got 2 + 3 = 5.	Writes 2 + 3 above 3 + 2 and says "All groups who got 2 + 3 = 5 circle it on your data table."
Did anyone spin another number sentence?	No.	
Do you think there are any other possibilities for 5?	Yes. 4 + 1 = 5.	Says, "That's true, but is it possible to spin a 1 using our spinners?"

Journal Prompt

Encourage students to write and make predictions in their journals about patterns they see in the number sentence chart as you write on the board. Discuss students' predictions.

The teacher continued to build the chart in this way. Students circled the number sentences on their data tables as the teacher wrote them on the board. The groups were excited about adding their sums to the chart. Each time the teacher wrote all the students' number sentences for a sum, she asked if there were any other possible ways to spin that sum. By using patterns found in the table, students were able to add to the chart any other possible number sentences that were not actually spun. For example, students could see that although no group had recorded 4 + 2 it still belonged on the chart since 2 + 4 was already included. When the class had listed all the possible combinations for the sums 4 through 8, the teacher asked if the students saw a pattern. (Refer to Figure 5.) Continue the discussion for sums 9 through 18.

Creating a Number Sentence Chart for Sums 9 through 18

Teacher Prompt	Student Response	Teacher Response
Do you see a pattern in our chart?	A: Yes, it keeps going up by one more. B: It goes up straight.	Right!
How many number sentences do we have for 7?	There are four ways to get 7.	
How many ways can we get 8?	Five.	
Good. Now, predict how many number sentences there will be for 9.	There will be one more. I guess there will be six ways to get 9.	Writes down the number sentences for 9 as the class tells them to her.
Were we right?	Yes!	
How many number sentences will there be for 10?	I bet there will be seven number sentences for 10.	Writes the number sentences for 10 as the students list them. Continues the same process for 11: asking the students for a prediction and then checking it. There are eight ways to get a sum of 11.
Predict the number of sentences for 12.	A: If the graph keeps going up, there will be nine. B: No, I think it's going to go down like it did on our graph. Eleven is in the middle. The highest points on our graphs were in the middle.	Says, "Okay, let's see if the graph will go up or down." Writes down the seven number sentences for 12. The graph begins to look like a pyramid.
You were right. The number of sentences for 12 was less than the number of sentences for 11. Predict the number of sentences with a sum of 13.	It will keep going down. There will be six number sentences.	Writes the six number sentences for 13, and then continues as before until the chart is complete.

Continue the class discussion by returning to **Question 3.** Using the graphs and class number sentence chart, students can now tackle this question. They should be able to see that spinning a seven is more likely than spinning an eighteen because there are four ways to get a sum of seven and only one way to spin the sum of eighteen.

Question 11 asks students to write a paragraph comparing the class chart to their group graph. Douglas wrote the following paragraph:

> Our graph looks like a mountain. The highest point is in the middle. The lowest points are at the sides and the ends. The difference between Our graph and the class graph is that our's is bumpy and theirs is strate. The highest point on their graph is eleven and the highest point on our graph is eleven.

Douglas did a great job describing the similarities and differences between the chart and the graph. However, he did not tell us why the graphs had the same highest point.

Journal Prompt

If you spin 40 more sums, what shape graph would you have? Why do you think so?

Discovery Assignment Book - page 22 *(Answers on p. 52)*

Math Facts

DPP Bit E provides practice with addition facts using doubles and with applying the same strategies to addition of larger numbers.

Homework and Practice

- Assign one or more of the Daily Practice and Problems items as homework for this unit. You can assign the problems, based on their difficulty, to different students or you can choose problems based on the subject matter.

- DPP items F, G, and H provide practice with money.

- Parts 1 and 2 of the Home Practice in the *Discovery Assignment Book* can also be assigned as homework. Both parts build number sense and mental math skills for addition and subtraction.

Answers for Parts 1 and 2 of the Home Practice are in the Answer Key at the end of this lesson and at the end of this unit.

Assessment

This activity provides an opportunity to assess students informally as they work with addition facts. As you observe each group, note whether students are able to find the sums quickly and accurately and whether they use appropriate strategies with difficult facts. For example, if you see that students are counting up from 9 to 17 in order to find 9 + 8, you may need to take time to review addition strategies for finding the sums quickly. Record your observations using the *Observational Assessment Record*. (See the TIMS Tutor: *Math Facts* in the *Teacher Implementation Guide* and Lesson 1 *Addition Facts Strategies*.)

At a Glance

Math Facts and Daily Practice and Problems

DPP Bit E provides practice with math facts. Items F, G, and H provide practice with money. Parts 1 and 2 of the Home Practice provide addition and subtraction practice.

Teaching the Activity

1. Discuss the activity using the *Spinning Sums* Activity Pages in the *Student Guide*, the *Spinners 2–9* and *Spinning Sums Data Table* Activity Pages in the *Discovery Assignment Book*, and the discussion prompts in the Lesson Guide.
2. Students spin the spinners forty times and record their number sentences in the *Spinning Sums Data Table*.
3. Students graph data from the table.
4. Students discuss and compare their group graphs.
5. Students answer *Questions 4–10* in the *Student Guide*.
6. As a class, students create and discuss a number sentence chart.
7. Students complete *Question 11* in the *Student Guide*.

Homework

1. DPP items may be assigned as homework.
2. Assign Home Practice Parts 1 and 2.

Assessment

Use the *Observational Assessment Record* to note students' abilities to use strategies to add quickly and accurately.

Answer Key is on pages 51–53.

Notes:

Name

Date

Horizontal Bar Graph, Blackline Master

Student Guide (p. 16)

Spinning Sums*

1. Answers will vary. 2 and 5; 3 and 4

2. 18

3. spinning a sum of 7

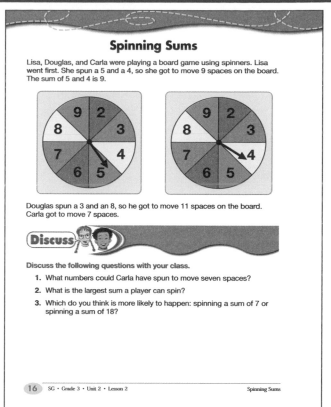

Student Guide - page 16

Student Guide (p. 17)

The following answers to *Questions 4–11* are based on the Spinning Sums graph in the *Student Guide*.

4. 11; the sum of 11 occurred seven times. The bar on 11 is the tallest.

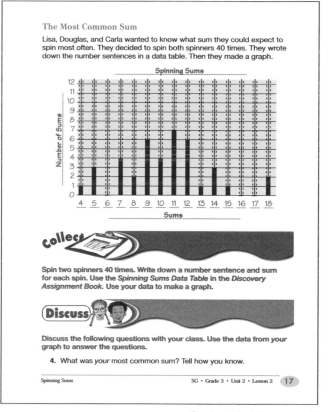

Student Guide - page 17

*Answers and/or discussion are included in the Lesson Guide.

5. What is *your* least common sum? Tell how you know.

6. Where are the tallest bars on your graph? What does it mean when the bars are tall?

7. Where are the shortest bars on your graph? What does it mean when the bars are short?

8. The graph Lisa, Douglas, and Carla made has taller bars in the middle. How does your graph compare?

9. Compare your graph to the other graphs in the class. How are they the same? How are they different?

10. Are the most common sums in the same place on all the graphs? What about the least common sums?

11. Write a paragraph comparing your graph to the class chart. Make sure you answer these questions:
   • How are your graph and the class chart alike or different?
   • Are the highest points on your graph and the class chart in the same place? What do they tell you?
   • Are the lowest points on your graph and the class chart in the same place? What do they tell you?

As a class, make a chart with all of the possible spins and sums.

18   SG • Grade 3 • Unit 2 • Lesson 2   Spinning Sums

Student Guide - page 18

Student Guide (p. 18)

5. 6, 16, and 17; the sums 6, 16, and 17 do not have bars on the graph.

6. In the middle; the sums in the middle are most common.

7. At either end; the sums on the ends are the least common.

8. Answers will vary.

9.–10. Answers will vary.
Similarities: The most common sums are clustered in the middle. The least common sums are clustered at both ends.

Differences: The most common sum for each group is not always the same, nor is the least common sum. Some groups may have 11 for the most common sum, while others have 10 or 12. Some groups have bars on every sum. Others have sums with no bars at all.

11. Answers will vary. See Lesson Guide 2 for a sample student paragraph.

Name _____ Date _____

Unit 2 Home Practice

PART 1

1. A. $18 - 10 = $ _____   2. A. $4 + 4 + 8 = $ _____
   B. $13 - 6 = $ _____   B. $7 + 9 + 8 = $ _____
   C. $14 - 9 = $ _____   C. $15 + 7 + 4 = $ _____

3. Kyle received eight new books for his birthday. He now has fifty-two books. How many books did Kyle have before his birthday? Show how you found your answer.

_____

_____

_____

PART 2

1. A. $15 + 5 + $ _____ $= 28$ B. $20 + 5 + $ _____ $= 28$
   C. $17 + $ _____ $+ 3 = 28$ D. $12 + $ _____ $+ 6 = 28$
   E. $5 + 9 + $ _____ $= 28$ F. $13 + 8 + $ _____ $= 28$

2. For the food drive, Ron's class collected seventeen cans of vegetables, four cans of fruit, and nine cans of soup.
   A. How many cans did they collect?

_____

   B. How many more cans of vegetables are there than soup?

_____

_____

22   DAB • Grade 3 • Unit 2   STRATEGIES: AN ASSESSMENT UNIT

Discovery Assignment Book - page 22

Discovery Assignment Book (p. 22)

Home Practice*

Part 1

1. **A.** 8
   B. 7
   C. 5

2. **A.** 16
   B. 24
   C. 26

3. 44 books; $52 - 8 = 44$ books

Part 2

1. **A.** 8   **B.** 3
   C. 8   **D.** 10
   E. 14   **F.** 7

2. **A.** 30 cans
   B. 8 cans

*Answers for all the Home Practice in the *Discovery Assignment Book* are at the end of the unit.

Discovery Assignment Book (p. 31)

Spinning Sums Data Table

Answers will vary. See Lesson Guide 2 for a sample
student data table.

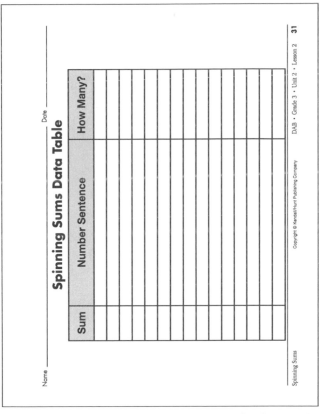

Discovery Assignment Book - page 31

Lesson 3

Yü the Great
A Chinese Legend

Lesson Overview

Estimated Class Sessions

1

Feng, a Chinese-American boy, asks his mother for help in arranging the digits 1 through 9 in a magic square. Feng's mother recognizes the problem as the ancient Chinese design called Lo-shu. At her son's request, she tells him the legend of the discovery of Lo-shu.

She tells the story of Emperor Yao, whose land is being ravaged by floods. Yao assigns Yü the task of taming the floods. Yü and his assistant, Yi, work for many years mapping the empire, deepening river channels and lakes, and building dams and dikes. On the banks of the river Lo, Yü and Yi see a giant turtle with a curious design on its back. The design is Lo-shu, the first magic square. Yü and Yi study the design and are inspired by symmetry and balance to create a Great Plan for the empire. Years later, Yü becomes the emperor.

Key Content

- Learning about the origin of magic squares.
- Appreciating the importance of mathematics (measurement, mapping, data gathering, and prediction) in human culture.
- Connecting mathematics and science with literature and social studies.

Key Vocabulary

- dikes
- Minister of Works
- taxes

Homework

Assign Parts 3 and 4 of the Home Practice in the *Discovery Assignment Book* for homework.

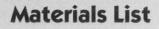

Materials List

Supplies and Copies

Student	Teacher
Supplies for Each Student	**Supplies**
Copies	**Copies/Transparencies**

All blackline masters including assessment, transparency, and DPP masters are also on the Teacher Resource CD.

Student Books
Yü the Great A Chinese Legend (*Adventure Book* Pages 12–25)

Daily Practice and Problems and Home Practice
DPP items I–J (*Unit Resource Guide* Page 22)
Home Practice Parts 3–4 (*Discovery Assignment Book* Page 22)

Note: Classrooms whose pacing differs significantly from the suggested pacing of the units should use the Math Facts Calendar in Section 4 of the *Facts Resource Guide* to ensure students receive the complete math facts program.

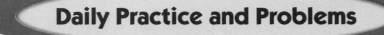
I. Bit: More Calculator Counting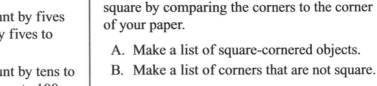
(URG p. 22)

Take turns counting and timing with a partner.

A. Predict how long it will take to count by fives to 100. Use a calculator to count by fives to 100. How long did it take?

B. Predict how long it will take to count by tens to 100. Use a calculator to count by tens to 100. How long did it take?

J. Task: Square Corners (URG p. 22)

Look around the classroom for corners that are "square." You can check to see if they are really square by comparing the corners to the corner of your paper.

A. Make a list of square-cornered objects.

B. Make a list of corners that are not square.

Yü the Great
A Chinese Legend

Adventure Book - page 12

Discussion Prompts

Content Note

According to Chinese tradition, Yü reigned from 2205 to 2197 BCE. He is the founder of the Hsia, or Xia, Dynasty, the first of the hereditary dynasties. No archaeological or direct literary evidence has yet been found for the Hsia, but most scholars consider the stories about Yü to have at least a kernel of truth. An active search is under way in central China today to uncover archaeological remains of this dynasty.

Page 12

The multicultural-historical perspective in this story relates mathematical processes to the contributions of an ancient culture. Opportunities for students to experience ancient methods for approaching problems are important. This perspective is intended to foster respect for the contributions of the groups involved.

This story is a companion piece to the next lesson, *Magic Squares*.

Page 13

Students will solve magic squares in the next lesson and in the Daily Practice and Problems (DPP). Specifically, they will solve the same puzzle that Feng confronts. This Adventure Book hints at the solution to this puzzle.

Adventure Book - page 13

Page 14

The story Feng's mother relates took place about 2200 BCE. You might want to ask your students how long ago this was.

Adventure Book - page 14

Adventure Book - page 16

Page 16

- *Why are units for length, volume, and mass important for building strong houses and trading fairly?*

People need to rely on *standard* units of measure when working collectively. Otherwise, the amount one person refers to will differ from the amount another person uses.

- *In the top picture, what are the people in the background doing?*

Using standard units to measure mass, volume, and length (from left to right).

Adventure Book - page 17

Page 17

The Chinese culture honors elders; therefore, the notion that a man could be better than his father is unusual.

Yü is modestly reluctant to take on the job. Many ancient Chinese legends have similar moralistic features.

- *What do you think the emperor, Yao, should do to stop the floods?*

Page 18

- *Why would making a map be a good first step toward controlling the floods?*

In order to prevent the flooding, Yü and Yi need to see the area as a whole. Where are the rivers, sea, swamps, and lakes in relation to the hills and lowlands? What natural features can they take advantage of as they create their plan?

- *What do the symbols on the map stand for?*

The symbols are the map key, and help the reader interpret the map correctly. This key shows the map's scale, mountains, swamps, lakes, and rivers.

The geographical names in the ancient sources are not the same as modern names. The Ho River is usually identified with the modern Yellow River, but this association is uncertain.

Adventure Book - page 18

Page 19

- *Yü and Yi are shown holding a T-square and a compass, tools used in mapping and construction work. Why might such tools be useful?*

These tools are helpful in making accurate drawings, such as those required in mapmaking and in construction plans.

Adventure Book - page 19

Adventure Book - page 20

Page 20

- *What purpose do you think the post with markings has?*

The post measures the water level. By recording the river's height periodically, Yü and Yi can gather data and find a pattern which would help them control the floods. Also, the rising water level would warn Yü and Yi if a flood were coming, allowing them to alert the nearby villagers. Even today, measuring the depth of rivers is an important part of flood control.

- *Could such markings really appear on a turtle's back?*

Up to this point, the story has been realistic, but now a fantastic element intrudes. Many traditional stories explain how something came to be. European fairy tales and the West African Anansi tales explain the origin of many natural phenomena. Although something about the turtle's appearance may have inspired Yü, it is not likely that there were clear markings on the turtle's back, as is depicted in this story. It is more likely that this story developed as a way to explain Yü's innovative thinking.

The Literature Connection following the Unit Outline contains a reference to another story that explains the origin of something—a string bean's seam.

Adventure Book - page 22

Page 22

- *Balance and symmetry are prominent in Lo-shu. What patterns can you find in the design?*

Students might find that all the middle groups in each row, column, and diagonal contain an odd number of circles and that all the corners contain an even number. The higher even numbers appear at the bottom of Lo-shu while the higher odd numbers appear at the top, balancing each other. There are many other patterns for your students to notice.

Page 23

- *The Great Plan was a design for organizing and governing the empire efficiently. What jobs do you think the government did to make the empire safe and prosperous?*

In the story, the government deepened the river and lake channels and built dams and dikes. It also regulated commerce. The Great Plan probably provided for many of the things our government provides for today: protection of its citizens from crime, good roads and bridges, and the resolution of disputes. To pay for this work, Yü's government taxed each region fairly.

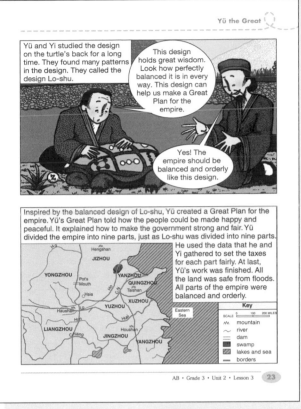

Adventure Book - page 23

Page 25

When the circles are translated into numbers, the figure gives a solution for a three-by-three magic square. This traditional magic square appears in DPP item T.

Adventure Book - page 25

PART 3

1. Does your kitchen table have square corners? How did you decide?

_____

_____

_____

2. Make a list of square-cornered objects that are in your home.

_____

_____

_____

PART 4

You go to the store to buy supplies. The prices are listed below. Explain your thinking for each problem.

eraser	30¢	folder	67¢
pencil	17¢	box of crayons	89¢
ruler	49¢	marker	42¢

1. You have one dollar. Can you buy a box of crayons and a pencil?

_____

_____

2. You have one dollar. Can you buy one marker, one folder, and a ruler?

_____

_____

_____

3. Your friend has $2. What can he or she buy?

_____

_____

_____

STRATEGIES: AN ASSESSMENT UNIT   DAB • Grade 3 • Unit 2   **23**

Copyright © Kendall/Hunt Publishing Company

Discovery Assignment Book - page 23 (Answers on p. 63)

Homework and Practice

- For DPP Bit I, students skip count by 5s and 10s to 100 using a calculator and record the time it takes for each. DPP Task J reviews the concept of a square corner (right angle).

- Assign Parts 3 and 4 of the Home Practice in the *Discovery Assignment Book* for homework.

Answers for Parts 3 and 4 of the Home Practice are in the Answer Key at the end of this lesson and at the end of this unit.

Literature Connection

- "The Straw, the Coal, and the Bean" from *The Complete Grimm's Fairy Tales*. Random House, Inc., New York, 1992.

Resources

- Chang, K.C. *Art, Myth, and Ritual*. Harvard University Press, Boston, 1983.

- Gernet, Jacques. *Ancient China from the Beginnings to the Empire*. University of Chicago Press, Chicago, 1968.

- Henderson, John B. *The Development and Decline of Chinese Cosmology*. Columbia University Press, New York, 1984.

- Sage, Steven F. *Ancient Sichuan and the Unification of China*. State University of New York Press, New York, 1992.

- Waltham, Clae. *Shu Ching: Book of History*. Henry Regnery Company, Chicago, 1971.

Discovery Assignment Book (p. 23)

Home Practice*

Part 3

1. Answers will vary. Students may use a corner of a sheet of paper to test for square corners.

2. kitchen table, books, floor tile, stove top, etc.

Part 4

1. No; explanations will vary. The crayons are almost 90¢. I would only have 10¢ left. The pencil is 17¢.

2. No; explanations will vary. The ruler and the marker each cost about 50¢ or two quarters. These two items alone would cost almost one dollar.

3. Answers will vary.

Name _____ Date _____

PART 3

1. Does your kitchen table have square corners? How did you decide?

_____
_____
_____

2. Make a list of square-cornered objects that are in your home.

_____
_____
_____

PART 4

You go to the store to buy supplies. The prices are listed below. Explain your thinking for each problem.

eraser	30¢	folder	67¢
pencil	17¢	box of crayons	89¢
ruler	49¢	marker	42¢

1. You have one dollar. Can you buy a box of crayons and a pencil?

_____
_____

2. You have one dollar. Can you buy one marker, one folder, and a ruler?

_____
_____
_____

3. Your friend has $2. What can he or she buy?

_____
_____
_____

STRATEGIES: AN ASSESSMENT UNIT   DAB • Grade 3 • Unit 2   **23**

Discovery Assignment Book - page 23

*Answers for all the Home Practice in the *Discovery Assignment Book* are at the end of the unit.

Lesson 4

Magic Squares

Lesson Overview

Magic squares are ancient number puzzles that have intrigued people for thousands of years. In this activity, students are introduced to magic squares by working on an easier, nontraditional type of magic square. These activities help develop problem-solving and addition skills.

Key Content

• Solving problems involving addition.
• Using patterns to solve problems.

Key Vocabulary

• magic square

Math Facts

Task L is a line math puzzle.

Homework

Assign the homework in the *Student Guide*.

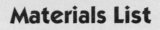

Materials List

Supplies and Copies

Student	Teacher
Supplies for Each Student • scissors • calculator	**Supplies**
Copies	**Copies/Transparencies** • blank transparency • 1 transparency of *Digits* (*Discovery Assignment Book* Page 33)

All blackline masters including assessment, transparency, and DPP masters are also on the Teacher Resource CD.

Student Books

Magic Squares (*Student Guide* Pages 19–21)
Digits (*Discovery Assignment Book* Page 33)

Daily Practice and Problems and Home Practice

DPP items K–L (*Unit Resource Guide* Page 23)

Note: Classrooms whose pacing differs significantly from the suggested pacing of the units should use the Math Facts Calendar in Section 4 of the *Facts Resource Guide* to ensure students receive the complete math facts program.

K. Bit: Pencils in the Classroom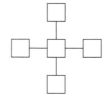
  (URG p. 23)

Estimate the number of pencils in your classroom
right now. Explain how you made your estimate.

L. Task: Line Math Puzzle (URG p. 23)

Put the digits 4, 5, 6, 7, and 8 in the boxes so that
the sum of each line is the same.

In this activity, students will work with digits cut out from the *Digits* Activity Page. Before they start to cut, have students color each row on the *Digits* Activity Page a different color. This way if the numbers get mixed up, they can be sorted by color.

Students should read the Adventure Book story, *Yü the Great.*

Before class, cut out the digits in at least the first rows of the transparency of the *Digits* Activity Page.

Teaching the Activity

Ask students to cut out the first row of the *Digits* Activity Page. Ask them to arrange these nine digits into a three-by-three square. Using the overhead or board, highlight a row, column, and main diagonal. Ask students to find the sums of each row, column, and main diagonal in their squares. Encourage students to show their squares and sums. Ask:

- *What are a few of the sums you found in your square?*
- *Did anyone arrange the squares so that all the sums are equal?*

If not, tell them to try to arrange the squares so that all the sums are 12. If students have difficulty with this challenge, suggest that they put 4 in the middle square.

- *Is there more than one arrangement?*

Invite other students to share their solutions. Figure 6 shows the four solutions.

6	2	4
2	4	6
4	6	2

Solution 1

4	6	2
2	4	6
6	2	4

Solution 2

2	6	4
6	4	2
4	2	6

Solution 3

4	2	6
6	4	2
2	6	4

Solution 4

Figure 6: *Four solutions*

Say:

- *If the digits are arranged so that all the sums are equal, then the square is called a **magic square.***

Discovery Assignment Book - page 33

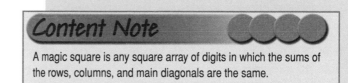

Content Note

A magic square is any square array of digits in which the sums of the rows, columns, and main diagonals are the same.

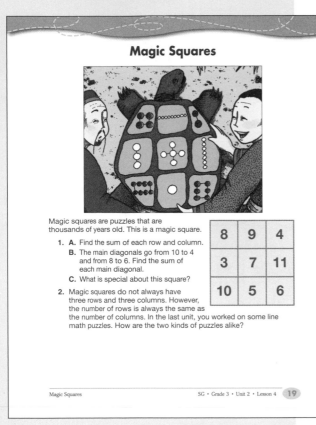

Magic Squares

Magic squares are puzzles that are thousands of years old. This is a magic square.

1. **A.** Find the sum of each row and column.
   B. The main diagonals go from 10 to 4 and from 8 to 6. Find the sum of each main diagonal.
   C. What is special about this square?

2. Magic squares do not always have three rows and three columns. However, the number of rows is always the same as the number of columns. In the last unit, you worked on some line math puzzles. How are the two kinds of puzzles alike?

8	9	4
3	7	11
10	5	6

Magic Squares   SG • Grade 3 • Unit 2 • Lesson 4 **19**

Student Guide - page 19 *(Answers on p. 71)*

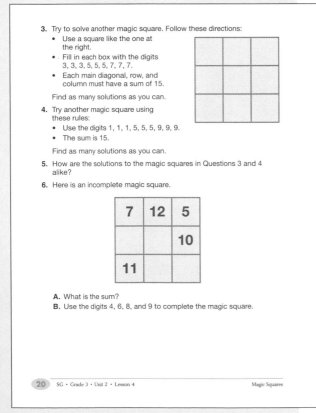

3. Try to solve another magic square. Follow these directions:
   - Use a square like the one at the right.
   - Fill in each box with the digits 3, 3, 3, 5, 5, 5, 7, 7, 7.
   - Each main diagonal, row, and column must have a sum of 15.

   Find as many solutions as you can.

4. Try another magic square using these rules:
   - Use the digits 1, 1, 1, 5, 5, 5, 9, 9, 9.
   - The sum is 15.

   Find as many solutions as you can.

5. How are the solutions to the magic squares in Questions 3 and 4 alike?

6. Here is an incomplete magic square.

7	12	5
		10
11		

   A. What is the sum?
   B. Use the digits 4, 6, 8, and 9 to complete the magic square.

20 SG • Grade 3 • Unit 2 • Lesson 4   Magic Squares

Student Guide - page 20 *(Answers on p. 71)*

If students did not find all four of the solutions, write them on the board and ask students to look for patterns. They may see that the fours are always along one of the main diagonals. Students might say that Solution 3 is like Solution 1 except that the twos and sixes are interchanged or that Solution 4 is like Solution 1 except that the first and last columns are swapped. Each row and each column has a two, a four, and a six.

Students may notice that magic squares bear a resemblance to the line math puzzles introduced in Unit 1. Line math puzzles are found in many shapes while magic squares are always squares.

Ask students to turn to the *Magic Squares* Activity Pages in the *Student Guide*.

Question 1 asks students to find the sum of each row, column, and main diagonal of a magic square. Figure 7 shows the solution.

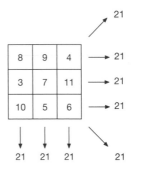

Figure 7: *The sum of each row, column, and main diagonal is 21.*

The magic squares in ***Questions 3*** and ***4*** are similar to the first magic square students created. The patterns they found with the first one can help them find solutions to ***Questions 3*** and ***4.*** An important pattern in these magic squares is that the three numbers on one of the main diagonals will be equal to the middle number on the list. Another pattern is that each row and column has one of each number. Students can use the *Digits* Activity Page and the blank magic square in the *Student Guide* to help them solve the magic squares.

Journal Prompt

Write your answer to ***Question 5*** in your journal.

Math Facts

DPP Task L is a line math puzzle and provides practice with math facts.

Homework and Practice

- Assign the *Magic Squares* Homework section in the *Student Guide*. Remind students to take home the two bottom rows from the *Digits* Activity Page to try out various arrangements.

- DPP Bit K is an estimation problem.

Extension

If some students complete their magic squares early, ask them to make a new 3 × 3 square by adding 3 to each of the nine numbers in their completed magic square for *Question 6.* Does this "ruin" the magic square by making the rows, columns, and main diagonals add up to different sums? What is the new sum? Try adding 5 to each of the nine numbers. What is the new sum? Try subtracting 2 from each of the nine numbers. What is the new sum?

⟨Homework⟩

Use the digits from the *Digits* Activity Page in the *Discovery Assignment Book*.

1. Try to solve a different magic square. Use these rules:
   - Use the digits 3, 3, 3, 6, 6, 6, 9, 9, 9.
   - The sum is 18.

   Find as many solutions as you can. Write your answers on a sheet of paper. Hint: Compare this magic square to those you created in Questions 3 and 4 during class.

2. Here is an incomplete magic square.
   A. What is the sum?
   B. Use the digits 7, 8, 9, and 11 to complete the magic square. Remember that each row, column, and main diagonal must have the same sum.

		13
14	10	6
	12	

3. Try to find another solution for a magic square. It should have the same sum as the one in Question 2. Begin with a blank magic square, and use the digits 6, 7, 8, 9, 10, 11, 12, 13, 14.

4. Here is another incomplete magic square.
   A. What is the sum?
   B. Use the digits 7, 9, 10, 12, 13, and 15 to fill in the blanks.

		8
	11	
14		

Magic Squares   SG • Grade 3 • Unit 2 • Lesson 4   21

Student Guide - page 21 *(Answers on p. 72)*

At a Glance

Math Facts and Daily Practice and Problems

DPP Bit K is an estimation problem. Task L is a line math puzzle.

Teaching the Activity

1. Students cut out the first row of the *Digits* Activity Page in the *Discovery Assignment Book* and arrange the nine digits into a three-by-three square.
2. Students find the sums of each row, column, and main diagonal.
3. Ask, *"What are a few of the sums you found in your square? Did anyone arrange the squares so that all the sums are equal?"*
4. Students arrange the squares so that all the sums are 12. (If students are frustrated, suggest that they put four in the middle.)
5. Students share solutions.
6. Introduce the idea of the magic square (all the sums are equal).
7. Write down all four solutions to this magic square and ask students to find patterns.
8. Students solve magic squares in the *Student Guide* using the *Digits* Activity Page.

Homework

Assign the homework in the *Student Guide.*

Extension

Have students who finish early add 3 to each box in their magic square. Ask questions such as: Does adding 3 to each box ruin the magic square? or What is the new sum? Then challenge students to add 5 or subtract 2 in each box and explore the results.

Answer Key is on pages 71–72.

Notes:

Student Guide (pp. 19–20)

Magic Squares

1. **A.** 21

   B. 21

   C. The sum of each row, column, and main diagonal is 21.

2. In line puzzles, each line has the same sum. In magic squares, each main diagonal, row, and column have the same sum.

3. The four solutions are listed below.*

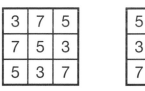

3	7	5
7	5	3
5	3	7

5	7	3
3	5	7
7	3	5

5	3	7
7	5	3
3	7	5

7	3	5
3	5	7
5	7	3

4. The four solutions are listed below.*

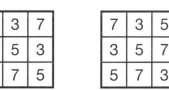

9	1	5
1	5	9
5	9	1

5	9	1
1	5	9
9	1	5

1	9	5
9	5	1
5	1	9

5	1	9
9	5	1
1	9	5

5. Answers will vary. The diagonals have the same middle number, 5. Each row and column has one of each number. The sums are the same. All the numbers are odd.

6. **A.** 24

   B.

7	12	5
6	8	10
11	4	9

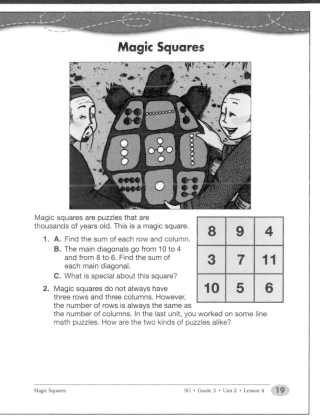

Student Guide - page 19

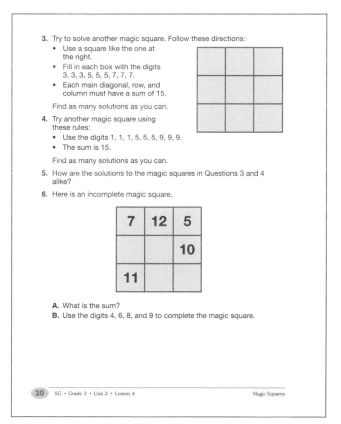

Student Guide - page 20

*Answers and/or discussion are included in the Lesson Guide.

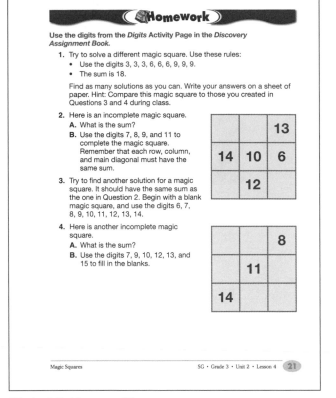

Student Guide - page 21

Student Guide (p. 21)

Homework

1. The following is one of four solutions.

3	9	6
9	6	3
6	3	9

2. **A.** 30

   B.

9	8	13
14	10	6
7	12	11

3. Answers will vary. There are 7 more solutions.

7	14	9
12	10	8
11	6	13

9	14	7
8	10	12
13	6	11

13	6	11
8	10	12
9	14	7

13	8	9
6	10	14
11	12	7

11	12	7
6	10	14
13	8	9

11	6	13
12	10	8
7	14	9

7	12	11
14	10	6
9	8	13

4. **A.** 33

   B. Answers will vary. There are 8 solutions in all. Two are shown below.

10	15	8
9	11	13
14	7	12

12	13	8
7	11	15
14	9	10

Lesson 5

Subtraction Facts Strategies

Lesson Overview

Estimated Class Sessions
2

This activity begins a review and practice of the subtraction facts. This focus will continue throughout the first half of the year. Students practice the facts as they encounter them in activities, labs, games, and the Daily Practice and Problems. Students' fluency is checked using quizzes in the DPP beginning in Unit 7.

The subtraction facts are organized by strategy into eight groups of nine facts. This lesson provides work with the first two groups of facts. These facts can be solved with the strategies using a ten, counting up, and thinking addition. Students will work with flash cards for these groups in Lesson 7. The additional six groups of facts will be introduced gradually through the Daily Practice and Problems. Appropriate strategies will be reviewed for each group.

Key Content

• Using strategies to learn subtraction facts.

Math Facts

DPP items N and O provide practice with math facts.

Homework

Students play *Nine, Ten* at home.

Assessment

1. Use DPP Task N to assess students' understanding of the Magic Square activity.
2. Use the *Observational Assessment Record* to note students' use of strategies to subtract.

Materials List

Supplies and Copies

Student	Teacher
Supplies for Each Student Pair • 2 clear spinners (or pencils and paper clips)	**Supplies** • 2 clear spinners
Copies	**Copies/Transparencies** • 1 transparency of *Spinners 11–18 and 9–10* (*Discovery Assignment Book* Page 35)

All blackline masters including assessment, transparency, and DPP masters are also on the Teacher Resource CD.

Student Books
Subtraction Facts Strategies (*Student Guide* Pages 22–27)
Spinners 11–18 and 9–10 (*Discovery Assignment Book* Page 35)

Daily Practice and Problems and Home Practice
DPP items M–P (*Unit Resource Guide* Pages 23–24)

Note: Classrooms whose pacing differs significantly from the suggested pacing of the units should use the Math Facts Calendar in Section 4 of the *Facts Resource Guide* to ensure students receive the complete math facts program.

Assessment Tools
Observational Assessment Record (*Unit Resource Guide* Pages 15–16)

Daily Practice and Problems

Suggestions for using the DPPs are on page 78.

M. Bit: 1 and 0 Are Broken (URG p. 23)

The "1" key and the "0" key are broken on the calculator. List the keys you would press to do these problems.

A. 10 + 10

B. 11 + 10

C. 11 + 11

O. Bit: Some Sums (URG p. 24)

Alex wrote the following number sentences to show six and seven broken into two parts.

$3 + 3 = 6$ $\qquad$ $6 + 1 = 7$

Write other number sentences to show six and seven broken into two parts.

N. Task: Magic Square: 4, 5, 6 (URG p. 24)

Complete the magic square using the digits 4, 4, 4, 5, 5, 5, 6, 6, and 6. Each row, column, and diagonal must have a sum of 15.

P. Task: Number Sentence Stories (URG p. 24)

Write a story for the following number sentence.

$25 = 19 + \underline{\quad}$

Student Guide - page 22

Student Guide - page 23

Part 1 Subtraction Facts Strategies

Subtraction Facts Strategies in the *Student Guide* begins with a discussion between John, Suzanne, and their teacher about three subtraction facts, $15 - 10$, $13 - 10$, and $15 - 9$. Through their discussion, students review subtraction facts strategies. After students read the two pages of dialog, ask questions like the following:

- *What strategy do you use to solve the problem $15 - 10$?*
- *John thinks facts with tens are the easiest. He solves two of them. What are other examples of facts with tens?*

After listing a few facts with tens on the board, ask:

- *What are the answers to these subtraction facts?*
- *What patterns do you see?*
- *Explain to a friend why John might think these are easy.*

Refer to Suzanne's explanation to introduce "facts with nines." Ask the class to generate a list of problems similar to $15 - 9$, such as $13 - 9$ or $17 - 9$.

Ask:

- *What is $13 - 9$? How did you solve it?*
- *Use Suzanne's method of counting up to do $13 - 9$.*
- *Describe how Suzanne "used a ten" to help her do $15 - 9$.*

Class discussion of strategies helps students verbalize number relationships and encourages them to think about the problems in new ways. It is important to emphasize that a strategy that works well for one person may not be helpful to another. The strategies mentioned here are suggestions students may find useful. Encourage students to develop and share their own strategies as well. They will encounter helpful strategies that will make learning the subtraction facts easier. Students who already demonstrate fluency with the facts may find that using a strategy is more work. Emphasize that these strategies will be more helpful when they solve problems such as $25 - 9$ or $33 - 19$.

Ask student pairs to discuss the questions in the *Student Guide.* It is not necessary for students to remember the names of the strategies, but to remember how to use them. Students may use different strategies to do the same problem. Pairs can report their answers and methods in a class discussion.

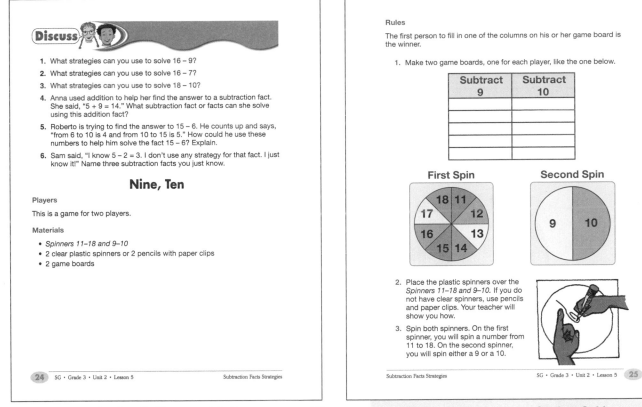

Discuss

1. What strategies can you use to solve 16 – 9?
2. What strategies can you use to solve 16 – 7?
3. What strategies can you use to solve 18 – 10?
4. Anna used addition to help her find the answer to a subtraction fact. She said, "5 + 9 = 14." What subtraction fact or facts can she solve using this addition fact?
5. Roberto is trying to find the answer to 15 – 6. He counts up and says, "from 6 to 10 is 4 and from 10 to 15 is 5." How could he use these numbers to help him solve the fact 15 – 6? Explain.
6. Sam said, "I know 5 – 2 = 3. I don't use any strategy for that fact. I just know it!" Name three subtraction facts you just know.

Nine, Ten

Players

This is a game for two players.

Materials

- *Spinners 11–18 and 9–10*
- 2 clear plastic spinners or 2 pencils with paper clips
- 2 game boards

Student Guide - page 24 *(Answers on p. 80)*

Rules

The first person to fill in one of the columns on his or her game board is the winner.

1. Make two game boards, one for each player, like the one below.

Subtract 9	Subtract 10

First Spin

18 11
17 12
16 13
15 14

Second Spin

9 10

2. Place the plastic spinners over the *Spinners 11–18 and 9–10*. If you do not have clear spinners, use pencils and paper clips. Your teacher will show you how.

3. Spin both spinners. On the first spinner, you will spin a number from 11 to 18. On the second spinner, you will spin either a 9 or a 10.

Student Guide - page 25

Journal Prompt

Describe a strategy you could use to help a friend find 17 – 9.

Part 2 Playing *Nine, Ten*

Students practice subtracting nine and ten while playing the game *Nine, Ten*. The game encourages the use of the strategies using a ten, counting up, and thinking addition.

Instruct students to read the directions for *Nine, Ten* in the *Student Guide*. As students play the game, circulate and listen to students as they solve the problems. If students are having trouble, encourage them to use strategies to help them write correct number sentences. Also, ask students to look for patterns on the game board as they fill in the columns. They may see that each difference in the "Subtract 10" column is the same as the ones digit of the first number in the sentence. They may also notice that each difference in the "Subtract 9" column is one more than the ones digit of the first number in the sentence.

4. Make a subtraction sentence with the two numbers you spin. Does your partner agree that your answer is correct? If so, write the number sentence in the game board column where it belongs. If it is not correct, do not write anything on the game board.

5. Take turns with your partner. The first player to fill in one of the columns on his or her game board is the winner.

Suzanne and John's Sample Game

Suzanne and John are playing *Nine, Ten*. Suzanne spins an 11 and a 9, so she says, "11 minus 9 equals 2." She answered correctly. She writes the number sentence in the column labeled "Subtract 9" on her game board.

Subtract 9	Subtract 10
11 – 9 = 2	

Now, it's John's turn. He spins an 18 and a 10. He says, "18 minus 10 equals 8." He answered correctly. He writes the number sentence in the column labeled "Subtract 10" on his game board.

Subtract 9	Subtract 10
	18 – 10 = 8

Student Guide - page 26

After playing a while longer, the game boards looked like this:

Suzanne's Board		John's Board	
Subtract 9	**Subtract 10**	**Subtract 9**	**Subtract 10**
11 – 9 = 2	17 – 10 = 7	18 – 9 = 9	18 – 10 = 8
17 – 9 = 8	15 – 10 = 5	13 – 9 = 4	12 – 10 = 2
15 – 9 = 6	11 – 10 = 1	18 – 9 = 9	13 – 10 = 3
18 – 9 = 9			16 – 10 = 6
			16 – 10 = 6

Notice that John recorded 16 – 10 = 6 twice. He spun the same numbers on two different turns. He answered the problem correctly both times. John completely filled in one column first. He won the game!

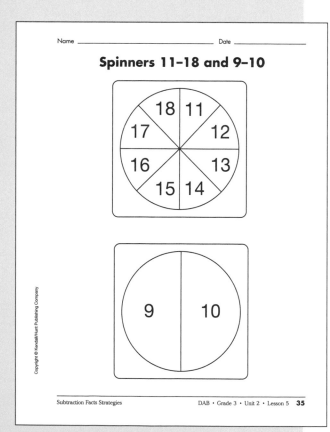

Play a game with a friend. Look for patterns in the number sentences on the game boards when you finish playing.

Subtraction Facts Strategies   SG • Grade 3 • Unit 2 • Lesson 5   27

Student Guide - page 27

Name _____ Date _____

Spinners 11–18 and 9–10

Subtraction Facts Strategies   DAB • Grade 3 • Unit 2 • Lesson 5   **35**

Discovery Assignment Book - page 35

Math Facts

DPP item O provides practice with addition facts.

Homework and Practice

- Students can play *Nine, Ten* at home with their families.
- DPP items M and P build number sense and computation skills.

Assessment

- A plan for assessing fluency with subtraction facts is discussed in the Daily Practice and Problems Guide and in Lesson 7.
- Use the *Observational Assessment Record* to note students' use of strategies to subtract.
- DPP Task N can be used as an assessment of the Magic Square activities.

Extension

Write the following problems on the board, and read them aloud.

$$\begin{array}{ccccc} 25 & 25 & 33 & 33 & 33 \\ -10 & -\ 9 & -20 & -19 & -14 \end{array}$$

Ask students to solve these problems in their heads. Guide students to the notion that the strategies can be generalized to two-digit numbers. Then discuss possible strategies for solving these problems.

Math Facts and Daily Practice and Problems

DPP items N and O provide practice with math facts. Items M and P build computation skills.

Part 1. Subtraction Facts Strategies

1. Students read *Subtraction Facts Strategies* in the *Student Guide.*
2. Discuss subtraction strategies. Students share their own methods.
3. Student pairs discuss *Questions 1–6* on the *Subtraction Facts Strategies* Activity Pages.

Part 2. Playing *Nine, Ten*

1. Students read the Nine, Ten section and the Suzanne and John's Game section in the *Student Guide.*
2. Student pairs play the game, discuss patterns, and share strategies.

Homework

Students play *Nine, Ten* at home.

Assessment

1. Use DPP Task N to assess students' understanding of the Magic Square activity.
2. Use the *Observational Assessment Record* to note students' use of strategies to subtract.

Extension

Write the following problems on the board and guide students to discover that strategies can be generalized to two-digit numbers.

$$
\begin{array}{ccccc}
25 & 25 & 33 & 33 & 33 \\
-10 & -\ 9 & -20 & -19 & -14 \\
\end{array}
$$

Answer Key is on page 80.

Notes:

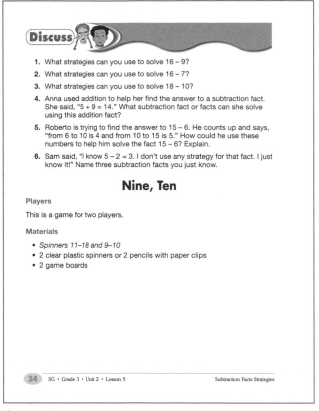

Student Guide - page 24

Student Guide (p. 24)

1. Answers will vary. Students may count up:
   From 9 to 10 is 1, from 10 to 16 is 6;
   $6 + 1 = 7$. Thinking addition: $9 + 7 = 16$
   so $16 - 9 = 7$. Using a ten: $16 - 10 = 6$
   so $16 - 9$ would be one more or 7. It is not
   necessary for students to remember the
   names of the strategies, but to remember
   how to use them.

2. Answers will vary. Counting up: From 7 to 10
   is 3, from 10 to 16 is 6; $3 + 6 = 9$. Thinking
   addition: $7 + 9 = 16$ so $16 - 7 = 9$. Using a
   ten: $16 - 6 = 10$ so $16 - 7$ would be one less
   or 9.

3. Answers will vary. Thinking addition:
   $10 + 8 = 18$ so $18 - 10 = 8$. Counting up:
   $10 + 8 = 18$. The answer is the second digit
   in 18 (the number in the ones place).

4. $14 - 9 = 5$; $14 - 5 = 9$

5. Answers will vary. Roberto can add the 4 and 5
   and get 9. $15 - 6 = 9$

6. Answers will vary.

Lesson 6 · Spinning Differences

Lesson Overview

Estimated Class Sessions

2

This assessment activity is similar to *Spinning Sums*. Students spin two spinners to generate random subtraction sentences and work in groups to answer the question, "Which is the most common difference?" They write descriptions about their solutions and problem-solving strategies.

Assess students' work based on their understanding of mathematical content. This is accomplished through the use of the Knowing dimension of the *TIMS Multidimensional Rubric* for teachers. The ideas in this rubric are written for students in the TIMS Student Rubric: *Knowing*.

Key Content

- Collecting, organizing, graphing, and analyzing data.
- Using patterns in data to make predictions and solve problems.
- Communicating solutions verbally and in writing.

Key Vocabulary

- difference
- rubric

Math Facts

DPP items Q, R, and T provide practice with math facts.

Assessment

Use the *TIMS Multidimensional Rubric* to score the activity, focusing on the Knowing dimension.

Curriculum Sequence

After This Unit

The Student Rubric: *Solving* will be introduced in Unit 5 of third grade. The Student Rubric: *Telling* will be introduced in Unit 7. The three rubrics, *Knowing, Solving,* and *Telling,* will be used to assess student work throughout third, fourth, and fifth grades.

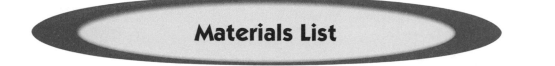

Materials List

Supplies and Copies

Student	Teacher
Supplies for Each Student Pair • 2 clear spinners (or pencil-paper clip substitute)	**Supplies**
Copies • 1 copy of *Spinning Differences* per student (*Unit Resource Guide* Page 90) • 1 copy of *Spinning Differences Data Table* per student (*Unit Resource Guide* Page 91) • 1 copy of *Horizontal Bar Graph* per student (*Unit Resource Guide* Page 50)	**Copies/Transparencies** • 1 transparency of *Spinners 2–9,* optional (*Discovery Assignment Book* Page 29) • 1 transparency or poster of Student Rubric: *Knowing* (*Teacher Implementation Guide,* Assessment section) • 1 copy of *TIMS Multidimensional Rubric* (*Teacher Implementation Guide,* Assessment section)

All blackline masters including assessment, transparency, and DPP masters are also on the Teacher Resource CD.

Student Books
Spinners 2–9 (*Discovery Assignment Book* Page 29), 1 per student pair
Student Rubric: *Knowing* (*Student Guide* Appendix A and Inside Back Cover)

Daily Practice and Problems and Home Practice
DPP items Q–T (*Unit Resource Guide* Pages 25–26)

Note: Classrooms whose pacing differs significantly from the suggested pacing of the units should use the Math Facts Calendar in Section 4 of the *Facts Resource Guide* to ensure students receive the complete math facts program.

Assessment Tools
TIMS Multidimensional Rubric (*Teacher Implementation Guide,* Assessment section)
Student Rubric: *Knowing* (*Teacher Implementation Guide,* Assessment section)

Daily Practice and Problems

Suggestions for using the DPPs are on page 88.

Q. Bit: What's Your Strategy? (URG p. 25)

Bill has trouble remembering the answer to $15 - 8$. What strategy might be helpful for Bill?

R. Challenge: Magic Square Mystery
(URG p. 25)

Complete the magic square using the numbers 5, 6, 7, 10, and 11. Each row, column, and diagonal must have the same sum. What is the sum?

9	4	
	8	
	12	

S. Bit: 1 and 2 Are Broken (URG p. 25)

The "1" key and the "2" key are broken on the calculator. List the keys you would press to do these problems.

A. $12 + 12$
B. $12 + 11$
C. $20 + 20$

T. Challenge: Magic Square: Sum = 15
(URG p. 26)

Complete the magic square using 1, 2, 3, 4, 5, 6, 7, 8, and 9. Each row, column, and diagonal must have a sum of 15. This is the same magic square that Sun Feng had to do in the story *Yü the Great*.

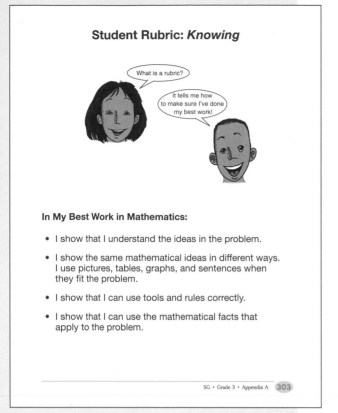

Student Rubric: *Knowing*

What is a rubric?

It tells me how to make sure I've done my best work!

In My Best Work in Mathematics:

- I show that I understand the ideas in the problem.

- I show the same mathematical ideas in different ways. I use pictures, tables, graphs, and sentences when they fit the problem.

- I show that I can use tools and rules correctly.

- I show that I can use the mathematical facts that apply to the problem.

SG • Grade 3 • Appendix A   303

Student Guide - Appendix A

Content Note

Larger numbers can be subtracted from smaller ones, yielding a negative result. Since students have not yet encountered negative numbers, they are likely to use the larger number first without instruction. Avoid advice such as "you can't subtract a larger number from a smaller one" since it may confuse students when they later encounter this situation.

Before the Activity

Have extra copies available of the *Spinners 2–9* Activity Page from the *Discovery Assignment Book* for Lesson 2 for students who have misplaced their own copies.

Teaching the Activity

This lesson introduces the TIMS Student Rubric: *Knowing.* (See the inside back cover of the *Student Guide.*) Post a copy of the rubric or show a transparency of it. If possible, make it part of a permanent bulletin board to remind students to use it and refer to it as needed. Discuss the rubric with students, making sure to spend time on each of the criteria. Explain that these criteria give them ideas about how to think about the math they are learning. By following the points of the rubric, they are better able to determine how well they know the math and how to show the math that they know. The rubric is a good tool for them to use to review and analyze their work.

Students need many experiences with the rubric. As their experience grows, they will become more comfortable applying the rubric to their work and the work of other students. Refer students to the rubric throughout the year.

To begin the assessment activity, present the class with the problem described on the *Spinning Differences* Assessment Blackline Master:

- *If you spin two spinners many times to make subtraction sentences, what will be the most common difference?*

Remind students that the **difference** is the answer to a subtraction problem. As students work in pairs to solve the problem, encourage them to use the Student Rubric: *Knowing* to guide their work.

The procedure for this activity is similar to *Spinning Sums.* However, students do not need to determine which spinner is first—they use the larger number as the first number in the subtraction sentence.

Distribute the assessment materials. Each individual student should have a copy of the *Spinning Differences* Assessment Blackline Master and the *Horizontal Bar Graph.* Each student pair should have a copy of the *Spinning Differences Data Table* Assessment Blackline Master, the *Spinners 2–9* Activity Page from Lesson 2, and two clear spinners. If you intend to place the data table in students' portfolios, make copies of the completed tables. Students should each make their own graph.

After you distribute the materials, your role in the students' process should be minimal. Let the pairs make their own decisions. They will have to decide how many times to spin the spinners, how to organize their data, and how to scale and label the graph. Once the pairs collect and record their data, they should discuss their results. Then each student should work independently to write a description about what he or she has learned.

Scoring the Assessment Activity

After students complete their work with *Spinning Differences,* talk about the criteria outlined in the Knowing dimension. Display transparencies of sample work from previous years or from the Lesson Guide and apply the rubric to them. Spend time discussing how the work does or does not reflect the goals defined in the rubric. This kind of discussion helps students learn how to apply the rubric and also helps them grasp mathematical content. Before you assign final scores for the assignment, comment on the first drafts and give students an opportunity to revise their work based upon your comments.

The following illustrates how one teacher scored student work for this activity. The teacher elected to focus on the Knowing dimension of the *TIMS Multidimensional Rubric.* (See the *Teacher Implementation Guide* for more information about the rubrics.)

Two students, Terrell and Hannah, completed *Spinning Differences* and turned in their work. The teacher reviewed the students' papers and wrote comments to focus the students' revisions. She also reminded them to use the *Knowing* rubric as a guide while they revised their work.

She reviewed the Knowing section of the teacher rubric and decided to look for the following:

- Were the data table and graph appropriately labeled?

- Was the graph scaled properly?

- Were the bars drawn correctly?

- Were subtraction sentences correct?

- Were the most common and least common differences identified?

Student work with teacher comments and grades are shown on the following pages in Figures 8 and 9.

Terrell's Work

The numbers tell what you can't go buy.

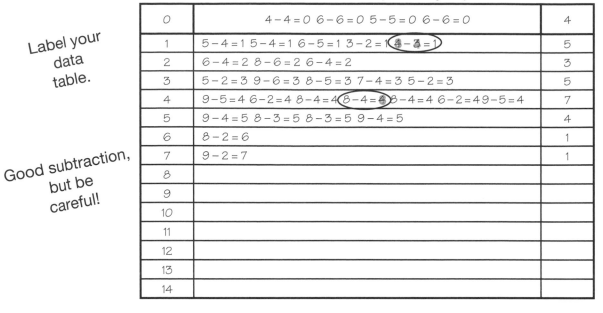

Label your data table.

Good subtraction, but be careful!

0	4 − 4 = 0 6 − 6 = 0 5 − 5 = 0 6 − 6 = 0	4
1	5 − 4 = 1 5 − 4 = 1 6 − 5 = 1 3 − 2 = 1 4 − 3 = 1	5
2	6 − 4 = 2 8 − 6 = 2 6 − 4 = 2	3
3	5 − 2 = 3 9 − 6 = 3 8 − 5 = 3 7 − 4 = 3 5 − 2 = 3	5
4	9 − 5 = 4 6 − 2 = 4 8 − 4 = 4 8 − 4 = 4 8 − 4 = 4 6 − 2 = 4 9 − 5 = 4	7
5	9 − 4 = 5 8 − 3 = 5 8 − 3 = 5 9 − 4 = 5	4
6	8 − 2 = 6	1
7	9 − 2 = 7	1
8		
9		
10		
11		
12		
13		
14		

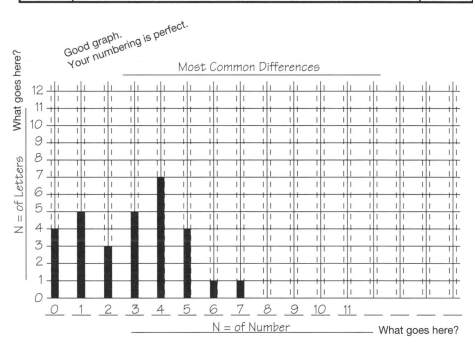

Good graph. Your numbering is perfect.

What goes here?

Most Common Differences

N = of Letters

N = of Number   What goes here?

Are graph looks like a truck. Because it looked like a truck. We had the most was four. Are least common was six and seven.

Your graph does look like a truck. How did you know what was the most likely difference? Where are the highest and lowest points on your graph?

Are lowest point was at the end. Are highest point was in the middle.

Figure 8: *Terrell's* Spinning Differences *work*

Hannah's Work

Difference	Spinning Differences	Totals
0	8 − 8 = 0, 5 − 5 = 0, 6 − 6 = 0, 7 − 7 = 0, 5 − 5 = 0	5
1	6 − 5 = 1, 6 − 5 = 1, 8 − 7 = 1, 6 − 5 = 1, 9 − 8 = 1	5
2	6 − 4 = 2, 5 − 3 = 2, 8 − 6 = 2, 6 − 4 = 4	4
3	5 − 2 = 3, 9 − 6 = 3, 9 − 6 = 3, 8 − 5 = 3, 9 − 6 = 3	5
4	7 − 3 = 4, 8 − 4 = 4, 6 − 2 = 4, 8 − 4 = 4, 6 − 2 = 4, 9 − 5 = 4	6
5	9 − 4 = 5, 9 − 4 = 5, 9 − 4 = 5, 9 − 4 = 5	4
6	9 − 3 = 6	1
7		0

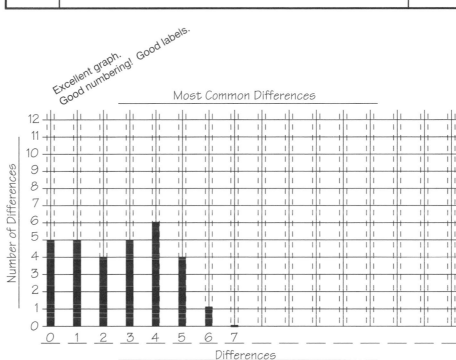

This is what the group graph looks like. The most common difference is four. The least common difference is seven. We decided that four was the biggest because it was the biggest bar. We decided that the smallest was seven. It looks like a roller coaster. That's what the group graph looks like.

Good paragraph. I like the way you told me how you decided on the most common difference. Where are the high and low points on your roller coaster?

The highest point is four. The lowest point is seven. Four is towards the middle. Seven is at the very end.

Figure 9: *Hannah's* Spinning Differences *work*

Terrell's Work

Refer to Figure 8 as you read this evaluation of Terrell's work.

Knowing, 3

Terrell's group decided to spin the spinners thirty times and collected appropriate data in the data table. Terrell wrote the subtraction number sentences, numbered the scales, and drew the bars on the graph correctly. He also identified the most common and least common differences correctly. However, the incorrect labels on both the data table and the graph indicate that he was unable to identify the important elements of the problem: the possible differences and the differences the group spun. Therefore, he was not clear on his goal for collecting the data.

Hannah's Work

Refer to Figure 9 as you read this evaluation of Hannah's work.

Knowing, 4

Hannah's group decided to spin the spinners thirty times and collected appropriate data in the data table. Hannah wrote the correct number sentences in the data table and also constructed and used the graph accurately. She was able to identify the numbers as differences and understood which was most common and least common. After receiving the teacher's comments about her first draft, Hannah correctly labeled her data table.

As part of Terrell's and Hannah's portfolios, their work can serve as a baseline for their progress.

Math Facts

DPP items Q, R, and T provide practice with math facts. For item Q, students choose and describe an appropriate strategy. Items R and T are variations on magic squares.

Homework and Practice

DPP Bit S develops number sense and computation skills.

Assessment

Use the *TIMS Multidimensional Rubric* and the Student Rubric: *Knowing* to assess students' abilities to use patterns in data to make predictions and solve problems and to communicate their mathematical reasoning.

At a Glance

Math Facts and Daily Practice and Problems

DPP items Q, R, and T provide practice with math facts. Bit S builds computation skills.

Teaching the Activity

1. Discuss the Student Rubric: *Knowing.*
2. Present the problem as described on the *Spinning Differences* Assessment Blackline Master.
3. Remind students that the **difference** is the answer to a subtraction problem.
4. Student pairs decide how they will solve the problem.
5. Student pairs collect data and organize the data on the *Spinning Differences Data Table* Assessment Blackline Master.
6. Students graph the data on a *Horizontal Bar Graph* and write a paragraph using the directions on the *Spinning Differences* Assessment Blackline Master. Remind them to think about the Student Rubric: *Knowing.*
7. Using samples of student work, conduct a class discussion about how to apply the rubric.
8. Comment on students' first drafts and give students the opportunity to revise.

Assessment

Use the *TIMS Multidimensional Rubric* to score the activity, focusing on the Knowing dimension.

Answer Key is on page 92.

Notes:

Spinning Differences

Problem

If you spin the spinners many times to make subtraction sentences, what will be the most common difference? Work with a partner to solve the problem.

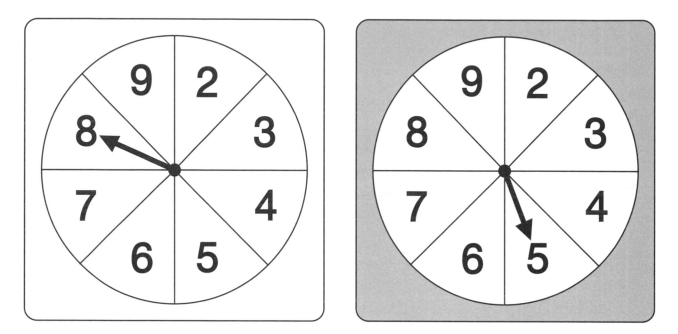

The subtraction sentence for this spin is 8 − 5 = 3.
The **difference** is 3.

What do you know about Spinning Differences? Write a paragraph that answers the following questions:

- **What is your group's most common difference?**

- **What is your group's least common difference?**

- **What did your group do to find the answer?**

- **How did you decide on your answer?**

Assessment Blackline Master

Name

Date

Spinning Differences Data Table

Assessment Blackline Master

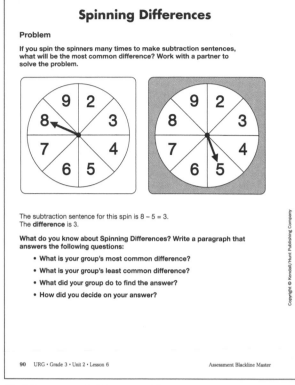

Unit Resource Guide (p. 90)

Spinning Differences

See Lesson Guide 6 for sample student work with teacher comments and grades.*

Unit Resource Guide - page 90

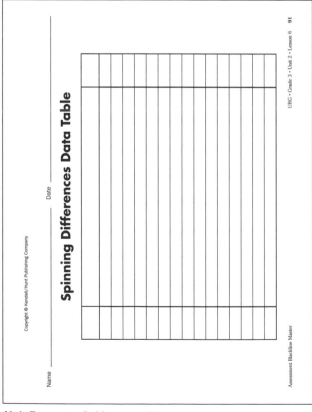

Unit Resource Guide (p. 91)

Spinning Differences Data Table

See Lesson Guide 6 for sample student work with teacher comments and grades.*

Unit Resource Guide - page 91

*Answers and/or discussion are included in the Lesson Guide.

Lesson 7

Assessing the Subtraction Facts

Lesson Overview

Estimated Class Sessions

1

To facilitate learning, the subtraction facts are organized by strategy into eight groups of nine facts each. This activity involves the first two groups of facts that can be solved with the strategies using a ten, counting up, and thinking addition. The other six groups of facts will be reviewed gradually through the Daily Practice and Problems. Students are assessed on their knowledge of the subtraction facts in three ways:

1. through teacher observation;
2. through student self-assessment; and
3. through the use of written quizzes and tests.

The assessment of students' fluency with the subtraction facts is closely aligned with the philosophy and organization of its instruction as described in the Background and Daily Practice and Problems Guide of this unit.

Key Content

- Assessing knowledge of the subtraction facts.

Math Facts

DPP Bit U provides practice with addition facts.

Homework

Students take home the flash cards for Group 1 and Group 2 to practice the subtraction facts with a family member.

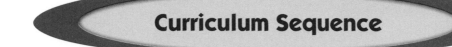

Curriculum Sequence

In Grade 2 Units 11–20 students practiced the subtraction facts using *Triangle Flash Cards*. After each time through the cards, they sorted them into three piles: those facts they knew quickly, those they knew using a strategy, and those they needed to study.

Students will continue to practice the subtraction facts in small groups in Units 3–10. They will take quizzes on these groups in Units 7–10. See Figure 10 for the distribution of the subtraction facts practice and assessment. See the Daily Practice and Problems Guide for this unit and the *Grade 3 Facts Resource Guide* for more information.

Materials List

Supplies and Copies

Student	Teacher
Supplies for Each Student • envelope for storing flash cards	**Supplies**
Copies • 1 copy of *Information for Parents: Grade 3 Math Facts Philosophy* per student (*Unit Resource Guide* Pages 13–14) • 1 back-to-back copy of *Subtraction Flash Cards: Group 1* per student, optional (*Unit Resource Guide* Pages 101–102) • 1 back-to-back copy of *Subtraction Flash Cards: Group 2* per student, optional (*Unit Resource Guide* Pages 103–104) **TIMS Tip** Copy each group of facts on different colored paper.	**Copies/Transparencies** • 1 transparency of *Subtraction Facts I Know,* optional (*Discovery Assignment Book* Page 43)

All blackline masters including assessment, transparency, and DPP masters are also on the Teacher Resource CD.

Student Books

Subtraction Flash Cards: Group 1 (*Discovery Assignment Book* Pages 37–38)
Subtraction Flash Cards: Group 2 (*Discovery Assignment Book* Pages 39–40)
Sorting Flash Cards (*Discovery Assignment Book* Page 41)
Subtraction Facts I Know (*Discovery Assignment Book* Page 43)

Daily Practice and Problems and Home Practice

DPP items U–V (*Unit Resource Guide* Page 26)

Note: Classrooms whose pacing differs significantly from the suggested pacing of the units should use the Math Facts Calendar in Section 4 of the *Facts Resource Guide* to ensure students receive the complete math facts program.

Daily Practice and Problems

Suggestions for using the DPPs are on page 100.

U. Bit: Addition Sentences (URG p. 26)

Write two addition sentences for each of the following sums.

A. 13   B. 17
C. 10   D. 11

V. Challenge: More Coins (URG p. 26)

List all the ways to make 40¢ without using pennies.

Students cut out Groups 1 and 2 of *Subtraction Flash Cards* so each student has eighteen flash cards for this activity.

Part 1 Strategies

Students discussed strategies for some of the subtraction facts from Groups 1 and 2 in Lesson 5. They can apply these strategies to the other facts in Groups 1 and 2. Write the following problems on the board or overhead: 13 − 4, 15 − 6, 14 − 5, and 16 − 7. Without referring to strategies, ask students for the answers to the facts. Then ask:

- *How did you solve 13 − 4?*
- *Could you use a ten or count up to help you solve 13 − 4? If so, describe how you would do so.* (Possible response: 13 − 3 is 10, so 13 − 4 is one less or 9.)
- *Could you use addition to help you solve the problem? If so, describe how you would do so.* (Since 4 + 9 = 13, 13 − 9 = 4.)

Part 2 Sorting Flash Cards

The eighteen facts in Groups 1 and 2 are grouped so students can use the subtraction strategies: using a ten, counting up, and thinking addition. Have student pairs put one deck of their flash cards away so they will not get mixed with those of their partners. Students will hold up one flash card at a time for their partner. Students use the *Sorting Flash Cards* Activity Page to sort the flash cards into three groups. If a student gives the correct answer quickly, then the flash card is laid on the first box labeled "Problems Answered Correctly and Quickly." If he or she answers correctly after thinking through a strategy, the flash card is laid on the second box labeled "Problems Answered Correctly after Thinking." If the student gives an incorrect answer, the flash card is laid on the third box labeled "Problems Answered Incorrectly."

After students finish sorting the flash cards, discuss the strategies they used to find the differences. Validate students' use of strategies unless they are inefficient. For example, if students are counting down from 15 to 9 by ones in order to solve 15 − 9, encourage them to replace this strategy with a more efficient one, such as using a ten. Class discussion of strategies helps students verbalize the number relationships and encourages them to think about the problems in new ways.

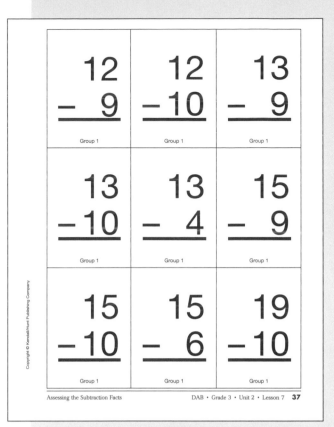

Discovery Assignment Book - page 37

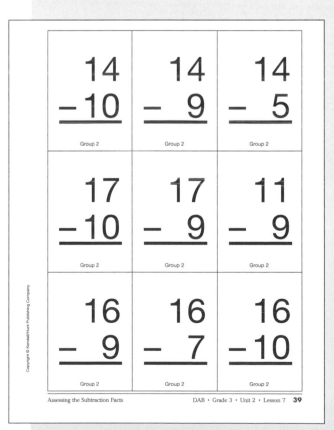

Discovery Assignment Book - page 39

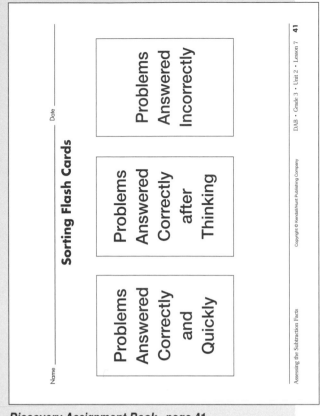

Discovery Assignment Book - page 41

After sorting the flash cards, students record their current fluency with subtraction facts on their *Subtraction Facts I Know* charts found in the *Discovery Assignment Book.* Using their piles on *Sorting Flash Cards,* students should:

- circle the facts corresponding to the cards in the stack labeled "Problems Answered Correctly and Quickly";
- underline the facts corresponding to the cards in the stack labeled "Problems Answered Correctly after Thinking";
- do nothing to the facts corresponding to the cards in the stack labeled "Problems Answered Incorrectly."

TIMS Tip

To reduce the number of lost flash cards, students should write their initials on the back of each flash card and store them in an envelope. These flash cards will be used many times.

For more durable flash cards, copy the flash cards onto card stock or laminate the cards. You can also give each student two sets of cards, so they can take a set home and leave a set at school.

Subtraction Facts I Know

Circle the subtraction facts you know and can answer quickly.
Underline those facts that you know when you use a strategy.
Do nothing to those facts that you still need to learn.

4 −2 = 2	5 −2 = 3	6 −2 = 4	7 −2 = 5	8 −2 = 6	9 −2 = 7	10 −2 = 8	11 −2 = 9
5 −3 = 2	6 −3 = 3	7 −3 = 4	8 −3 = 5	9 −3 = 6	10 −3 = 7	11 −3 = 8	12 −3 = 9
6 −4 = 2	7 −4 = 3	8 −4 = 4	9 −4 = 5	10 −4 = 6	11 −4 = 7	12 −4 = 8	13 −4 = 9
7 −5 = 2	8 −5 = 3	9 −5 = 4	10 −5 = 5	11 −5 = 6	12 −5 = 7	13 −5 = 8	14 −5 = 9
8 −6 = 2	9 −6 = 3	10 −6 = 4	11 −6 = 5	12 −6 = 6	13 −6 = 7	14 −6 = 8	15 −6 = 9
9 −7 = 2	10 −7 = 3	11 −7 = 4	12 −7 = 5	13 −7 = 6	14 −7 = 7	15 −7 = 8	16 −7 = 9
10 −8 = 2	11 −8 = 3	12 −8 = 4	13 −8 = 5	14 −8 = 6	15 −8 = 7	16 −8 = 8	17 −8 = 9
11 −9 = 2	12 −9 = 3	13 −9 = 4	14 −9 = 5	15 −9 = 6	16 −9 = 7	17 −9 = 8	18 −9 = 9
12 −10 = 2	13 −10 = 3	14 −10 = 4	15 −10 = 5	16 −10 = 6	17 −10 = 7	18 −10 = 8	19 −10 = 9

Discovery Assignment Book - page 43

As students encounter all eight groups of facts in the Daily Practice and Problems, they should update their information on the chart by circling those problems they learn to answer quickly and underlining those facts they answer correctly after thinking.

To acquaint students with the *Subtraction Facts I Know* chart, ask students to look for patterns. Possible patterns include:

- the top numbers in each row get larger as you read from left to right;
- the top numbers in each column get larger as you read from top to bottom;
- all the subtraction facts that begin with eleven are in a diagonal that begins at the top right corner;
- the number to be subtracted is the same throughout each row, beginning with the 2 row, continuing with the 3 row, and so on;
- the differences increase by one as you read from left to right in each row.

Students can also refer to their *Subtraction Facts I Know* charts for facts they do not know as they encounter them in activities or labs. Students will see the number of facts that are circled or underlined grow as they learn more efficient strategies for finding the answers and as they use and practice the facts in activities, labs, and games.

Notes about Written Quizzes and Tests

There are four quizzes, each of which has eighteen subtraction facts. These quizzes are located in the DPP in Units 7–10 as shown in Figure 10.

In addition to these short quizzes, there is an inventory test of all seventy-two facts in Unit 10. This test is provided as part of the midyear assessments. More frequent testing may cause frustration or send the message that math is merely rote memorization of facts.

The Teacher Notes in the Daily Practice and Problems will remind you when to administer each quiz and the inventory test. Good performance on these assessments, however, is not a prerequisite for learning more complex mathematics. To solve more sophisticated problems, students can use strategies, manipulatives, calculators, or their *Subtraction Facts I Know* charts if they have difficulties.

Fluency with the subtraction facts will be maintained through the distributed practice outlined above and through the use of math facts in solving problems.

Unit	Groups	Discussion Strategies	Distribution of Quizzes
2	1 and 2	Using a Ten, Thinking Addition	
3	3 and 4	Making a Ten	
4	5	Counting Strategies	
	6	Thinking Addition	
5	7 and 8	Using Doubles	
7	1 and 2	Using a Ten, Thinking Addition	A
8	3 and 4	Making a Ten	B
9	5	Counting Strategies	C
	6	Thinking Addition	
10	7 and 8	Using Doubles	D

Figure 10: *Subtraction Facts Practice and Assessment for Units 2–10*

Math Facts

DPP Bit U provides practice with addition facts.

Homework and Practice

- Students can take home the flash cards for Group 1 and Group 2 to practice.
- DPP Challenge V provides practice with money.

Estimated Class Sessions

1

At a Glance

Math Facts and Daily Practice and Problems

DPP Bit U provides practice with addition facts. Challenge V is a money problem.

Part 1. Strategies

Students discuss strategies for solving subtraction facts.

Part 2. Sorting Flash Cards

1. Students work in pairs to practice the subtraction facts in Group 1 and Group 2 using flash cards.
2. After going through all the cards, students sort the cards into three categories on the *Sorting Flash Cards* Activity Page.

Part 3. Subtraction Facts I Know

1. Students record their fluency with subtraction facts on the *Subtraction Facts I Know* chart.
2. Students update this chart throughout the year.

Homework

Students take home the flash cards for Group 1 and Group 2 to practice the subtraction facts with a family member.

Notes:

12 − 9 Group 1	12 − 10 Group 1	13 − 9 Group 1
13 − 10 Group 1	13 − 4 Group 1	15 − 9 Group 1
15 − 10 Group 1	15 − 6 Group 1	19 − 10 Group 1

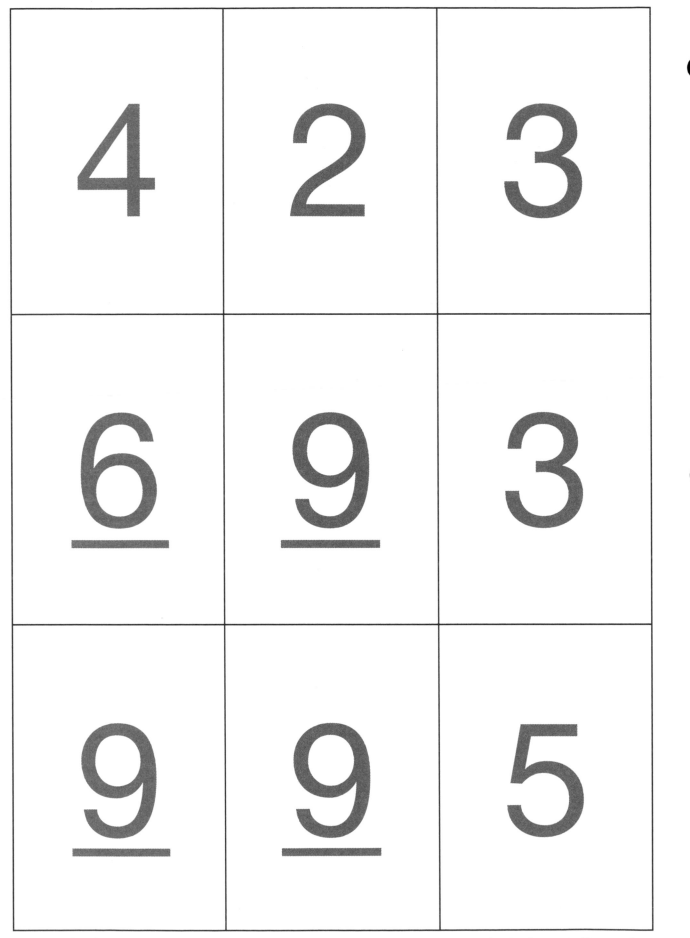

Subtraction Flash Cards: Group 1—Reverse Side

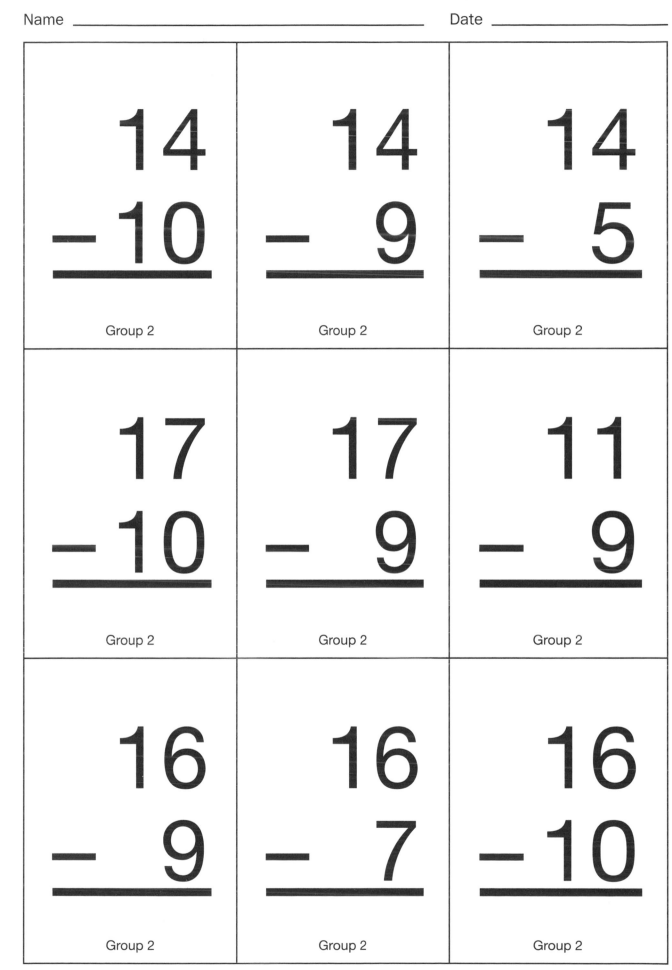

14
− 10
_____
Group 2

14
− 9
_____
Group 2

14
− 5
_____
Group 2

17
− 10
_____
Group 2

17
− 9
_____
Group 2

11
− 9
_____
Group 2

16
− 9
_____
Group 2

16
− 7
_____
Group 2

16
− 10
_____
Group 2

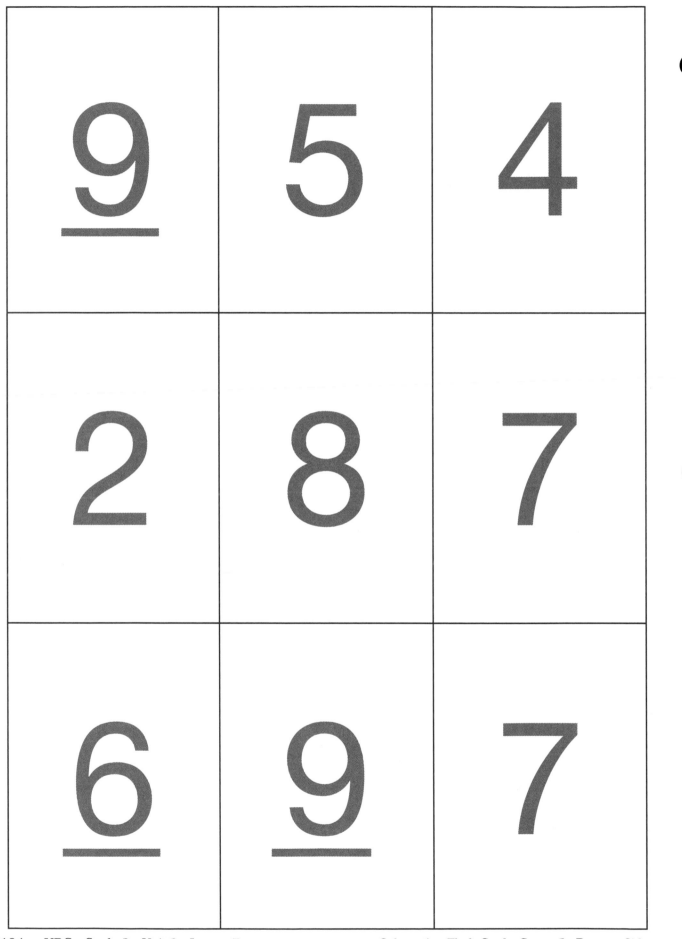

Subtraction Flash Cards: Group 2—Reverse Side

Number Sense with Dollars and Cents

Lesson Overview

Estimated Class Sessions

1

Students work with a list of items and their prices. They estimate which items they can buy for a given amount of money.

Key Content

- Solving problems involving money.
- Developing number sense.
- Estimating prices.

Assessment

1. Use the *Observational Assessment Record* to document students' abilities to verbally communicate mathematical reasoning.
2. Transfer appropriate assessment documentation from the Unit 2 *Observational Assessment Record* to students' *Individual Assessment Record Sheets*.

Materials List

Supplies and Copies

Student	Teacher
Supplies for Each Student	**Supplies**
Copies	**Copies/Transparencies**

All blackline masters including assessment, transparency, and DPP masters are also on the Teacher Resource CD.

Student Books
Number Sense with Dollars and Cents (*Student Guide* Pages 28–29)

Daily Practice and Problems and Home Practice
DPP items W–X (*Unit Resource Guide* Page 27)

Note: Classrooms whose pacing differs significantly from the suggested pacing of the units should use the Math Facts Calendar in Section 4 of the *Facts Resource Guide* to ensure students receive the complete math facts program.

Assessment Tools
Observational Assessment Record (*Unit Resource Guide* Pages 15–16)
Individual Assessment Record Sheet (*Teacher Implementation Guide,* Assessment section)

Daily Practice and Problems

Suggestions for using the DPPs are on page 109.

W. Bit: Fruit for $2 (URG p. 27) $\boxed{\$}$ $\boxed{N}$ $\boxed{\times}$

These are the fruit prices at Fred's Fantastic Fruit Farm. You have $2 to spend.

Apples	33¢ each
Apple Cider	75¢ per quart
Pears	50¢ each
Grapes	65¢ a bunch
Plums	24¢ each

1. Can you buy four pears? Why or why not?
2. Can you buy eight plums? Why or why not?
3. Can you buy four bunches of grapes? Why or why not?

X. Task: More Fruit for $2 $\boxed{N}$ $\boxed{\times}$ $\boxed{\$}$
(URG p. 27)

These are the fruit prices at Fred's Fantastic Fruit Farm. You have $2 to spend.

Apples	33¢ each
Apple Cider	75¢ per quart
Pears	50¢ each
Grapes	65¢ a bunch
Plums	24¢ each

Figure out these problems in your head:

A. Can you buy an apple, one bunch of grapes, and a quart of apple cider?

B. What would you buy for $2?

Number Sense with Dollars and Cents

Student Guide - page 28

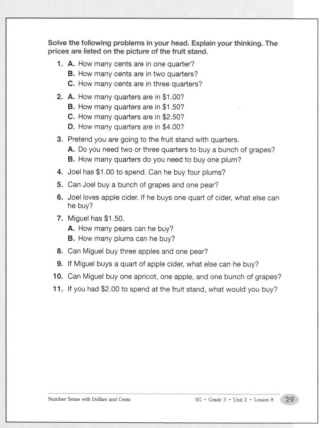

Solve the following problems in your head. Explain your thinking. The prices are listed on the picture of the fruit stand.

1. **A.** How many cents are in one quarter?
   B. How many cents are in two quarters?
   C. How many cents are in three quarters?

2. **A.** How many quarters are in $1.00?
   B. How many quarters are in $1.50?
   C. How many quarters are in $2.50?
   D. How many quarters are in $4.00?

3. Pretend you are going to the fruit stand with quarters.
   A. Do you need two or three quarters to buy a bunch of grapes?
   B. How many quarters do you need to buy one plum?

4. Joel has $1.00 to spend. Can he buy four plums?

5. Can Joel buy a bunch of grapes and one pear?

6. Joel loves apple cider. If he buys one quart of cider, what else can he buy?

7. Miguel has $1.50.
   A. How many pears can he buy?
   B. How many plums can he buy?

8. Can Miguel buy three apples and one pear?

9. If Miguel buys a quart of apple cider, what else can he buy?

10. Can Miguel buy one apricot, one apple, and one bunch of grapes?

11. If you had $2.00 to spend at the fruit stand, what would you buy?

Student Guide - page 29 (Answers on p. 111)

Teaching the Activity

Ask students to skip count by 25¢ to $3.00. Write the prices on the board as they skip count: 25¢, 50¢, 75¢, $1.00, $1.25, and so on. Also ask them to skip count by 50¢ to $5.00.

On the board, list the items and their prices from the picture on the first *Number Sense with Dollars and Cents* Activity Page in the *Student Guide.* Have student pairs discuss **Questions 1–3.** Encourage them to answer the questions without paper and pencil. After several minutes, ask students to report their solutions and strategies.

The first three questions help prepare students to use benchmarks (such as 25¢ and 50¢) when estimating answers for **Questions 4–10** and when solving similar problems throughout the year. Recommendations such as "think of quarters," "use convenient numbers like 25¢ or 50¢," or "skip count by quarters" may be helpful.

Encourage students to develop their own strategies as they solve **Questions 4–10** in pairs or groups. Remind students that they need not find the exact total cost of the fruit in order to solve the problems. Rather, they need to find an approximate cost so they can determine if the purchase can be made. After students solve the problems, discuss their solution strategies. A few examples of solution strategies are provided.

Another helpful strategy, doubling, can be used for **Question 4.**

> Joel can buy four plums. If I double 24 cents, that is 48 cents—less than 50 cents. So if I double it again, the price will still be less than one dollar.

To solve **Question 5,** using a benchmark of 50 cents is helpful.

> Since a pear costs almost 50 cents and a bunch of grapes costs a good bit more than 50 cents, Joel will not be able to buy both for one dollar.

Let the students teach one another through discussion.

Some or all of these problems can be assigned for homework. This is an appropriate activity to leave for a substitute teacher.

DPP items W and X provide similar fruit stand problems requiring estimation.

- Use the *Observational Assessment Record* to note students' abilities to verbally communicate mathematical reasoning.

- Transfer appropriate assessment documentation from the Unit 2 *Observational Assessment Record* to students' *Individual Assessment Record Sheets.*

Estimated Class Sessions

1

At a Glance

Math Facts and Daily Practice and Problems

DPP items W and X provide additional practice estimating prices.

Teaching the Activity

1. List the items and prices from the first *Number Sense with Dollars and Cents* Activity Page.
2. Ask students to solve *Questions 1–3.*
3. Discuss their answers and solution strategies.
4. Ask students to solve *Questions 4–10.* Encourage the use of benchmarks such as 25¢ and 50¢.
5. Students share their solutions and solution strategies.

Assessment

1. Use the *Observational Assessment Record* to document students' abilities to verbally communicate mathematical reasoning.
2. Transfer appropriate assessment documentation from the Unit 2 *Observational Assessment Record* to students' *Individual Assessment Record Sheets.*

Answer Key is on page 111.

Notes:

Student Guide (p. 29)

Solution strategies will vary.*

1. **A.** 25¢

   B. 50¢

   C. 75¢

2. **A.** 4

   B. 6

   C. 10

   D. 16

3. **A.** 3 quarters

   B. 1 quarter

4. Yes. If each plum were 25¢ he could buy 4. Each is less than 25¢.

5. No. One pear is 50¢. A bunch of grapes is more than 50¢. The cost of both would be more than a dollar.

6. one plum

7. **A.** 3 pears

   B. 6 plums

8. Yes. Three apples cost less than one dollar. A pear costs 50¢. The cost of both would be less than $1.50.

9. Answers will vary. One pear and one plum; one apple and one apricot; one plum and one apricot.

10. Yes. One bunch of grapes and one apple cost less than $1.00. An apricot is less than 50¢.

11. Answers will vary.

Solve the following problems in your head. Explain your thinking. The prices are listed on the picture of the fruit stand.

1. **A.** How many cents are in one quarter?
    B. How many cents are in two quarters?
    C. How many cents are in three quarters?

2. **A.** How many quarters are in $1.00?
    B. How many quarters are in $1.50?
    C. How many quarters are in $2.50?
    D. How many quarters are in $4.00?

3. Pretend you are going to the fruit stand with quarters.
    A. Do you need two or three quarters to buy a bunch of grapes?
    B. How many quarters do you need to buy one plum?

4. Joel has $1.00 to spend. Can he buy four plums?

5. Can Joel buy a bunch of grapes and one pear?

6. Joel loves apple cider. If he buys one quart of cider, what else can he buy?

7. Miguel has $1.50.
    A. How many pears can he buy?
    B. How many plums can he buy?

8. Can Miguel buy three apples and one pear?

9. If Miguel buys a quart of apple cider, what else can he buy?

10. Can Miguel buy one apricot, one apple, and one bunch of grapes?

11. If you had $2.00 to spend at the fruit stand, what would you buy?

Number Sense with Dollars and Cents   SG • Grade 3 • Unit 2 • Lesson 8   **29**

Student Guide - page 29

*Answers and/or discussion are included in the Lesson Guide.

Name _____ Date _____

Unit 2 Home Practice

PART 1

1. A. 18 – 10 = _____
   B. 13 – 6 = _____
   C. 14 – 9 = _____

2. A. 4 + 4 + 8 = _____
   B. 7 + 9 + 8 = _____
   C. 15 + 7 + 4 = _____

3. Kyle received eight new books for his birthday. He now has fifty-two books. How many books did Kyle have before his birthday? Show how you found your answer.

   _____
   _____
   _____
   _____

PART 2

1. A. 15 + 5 + _____ = 28
   C. 17 + _____ + 3 = 28
   E. 5 + 9 + _____ = 28
   B. 20 + 5 + _____ = 28
   D. 12 + _____ + 6 = 28
   F. 13 + 8 + _____ = 28

2. For the food drive, Ron's class collected seventeen cans of vegetables, four cans of fruit, and nine cans of soup.
   A. How many cans did they collect?

   _____
   _____

   B. How many more cans of vegetables are there than soup?

   _____
   _____

Discovery Assignment Book - page 22

Discovery Assignment Book (p. 22)

Part 1

1. A. 8
   B. 7
   C. 5

2. A. 16
   B. 24
   C. 26

3. 44 books; $52 - 8 = 44$ books

Part 2

1. A. 8   B. 3
   C. 8   D. 10
   E. 14   F. 7

2. A. 30 cans   B. 8 cans

Name _____ Date _____

PART 3

1. Does your kitchen table have square corners? How did you decide?

   _____
   _____
   _____

2. Make a list of square-cornered objects that are in your home.

   _____
   _____
   _____

PART 4

You go to the store to buy supplies. The prices are listed below. Explain your thinking for each problem.

eraser	30¢	folder	67¢
pencil	17¢	box of crayons	89¢
ruler	49¢	marker	42¢

1. You have one dollar. Can you buy a box of crayons and a pencil?

   _____
   _____

2. You have one dollar. Can you buy one marker, one folder, and a ruler?

   _____
   _____
   _____

3. Your friend has $2. What can he or she buy?

   _____
   _____
   _____

Discovery Assignment Book - page 23

Discovery Assignment Book (p. 23)

Part 3

1. Answers will vary. Students may use a corner of a sheet of paper to test for square corners.

2. kitchen table, books, floor tile, stove top, etc.

Part 4

1. No; explanations will vary. The crayons are almost 90¢. I would only have 10¢ left. The pencil is 17¢.

2. No; explanations will vary. The ruler and the marker each cost about 50¢ or two quarters. These two items alone would cost almost one dollar.

3. Answers will vary.

Glossary

This glossary provides definitions of key vocabulary terms in the Grade 3 lessons. Locations of key vocabulary terms in the curriculum are included with each definition. Components Key: URG = *Unit Resource Guide,* SG = *Student Guide,* and DAB = *Discovery Assignment Book.*

A

Area (URG Unit 5; SG Unit 5)
The area of a shape is the amount of space it covers, measured in square units.

Array (URG Unit 7 & Unit 11)
An array is an arrangement of elements into a rectangular pattern of (horizontal) rows and (vertical) columns. (*See* column and row.)

Associative Property of Addition (URG Unit 2)
For any three numbers a, b, and c we have $a + (b + c) = (a + b) + c$. For example in finding the sum of 4, 8, and 2, one can compute $4 + 8$ first and then add 2: $(4 + 8) + 2 = 14$. Alternatively, we can compute $8 + 2$ and then add the result to 4: $4 + (8 + 2) = 4 + 10 = 14$.

Average (URG Unit 5)
A number that can be used to represent a typical value in a set of data. (*See also* mean and median.)

Axes (URG Unit 8; SG Unit 8)
Reference lines on a graph. In the Cartesian coordinate system, the axes are two perpendicular lines that meet at the origin. The singular of axes is axis.

B

Base (of a cube model) (URG Unit 18; SG Unit 18)
The part of a cube model that sits on the "ground."

Base-Ten Board (URG Unit 4)
A tool to help children organize base-ten pieces when they are representing numbers.

Base-Ten Pieces (URG Unit 4; SG Unit 4)
A set of manipulatives used to model our number system as shown in the figure at the right. Note that a skinny is made of 10 bits, a flat is made of 100 bits, and a pack is made of 1000 bits.

Base-Ten Shorthand (SG Unit 4)
A pictorial representation of the base-ten pieces as shown.

Nickname	Picture	Shorthand
bit		·
skinny		/
flat		
pack		

Best-Fit Line (URG Unit 9; SG Unit 9; DAB Unit 9)
The line that comes closest to the most number of points on a point graph.

Bit (URG Unit 4; SG Unit 4)
A cube that measures 1 cm on each edge. It is the smallest of the base-ten pieces that is often used to represent 1. (*See also* base-ten pieces.)

C

Capacity (URG Unit 16)
1. The volume of the inside of a container.
2. The largest volume a container can hold.

Cartesian Coordinate System (URG Unit 8)
A method of locating points on a flat surface by means of numbers. This method is named after its originator, René Descartes. (*See also* coordinates.)

Centimeter (cm)
A unit of measure in the metric system equal to one-hundredth of a meter. (1 inch = 2.54 cm)

Column (URG Unit 11)
In an array, the objects lined up vertically.

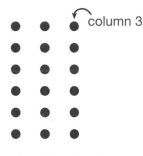
column 3

Common Fraction (URG Unit 15)
Any fraction that is written with a numerator and denominator that are whole numbers. For example, $\frac{3}{4}$ and $\frac{9}{4}$ are both common fractions. (*See also* decimal fraction.)

Commutative Property of Addition (URG Unit 2 & Unit 11)
This is also known as the Order Property of Addition. Changing the order of the addends does not change the sum. For example, $3 + 5 = 5 + 3 = 8$. Using variables, $n + m = m + n$.

Commutative Property of Multiplication (URG Unit 11)
Changing the order of the factors in a multiplication problem does not change the result, e.g., $7 \times 3 = 3 \times 7 = 21$. (*See also* turn-around facts.)

Congruent (URG Unit 12 & Unit 17; SG Unit 12)
Figures with the same shape and size.

Convenient Number (URG Unit 6)
A number used in computation that is close enough to give a good estimate, but is also easy to compute mentally, e.g., 25 and 30 are convenient numbers for 27.

Coordinates (URG Unit 8; SG Unit 8)
An ordered pair of numbers that locates points on a flat surface by giving distances from a pair of coordinate axes. For example, if a point has coordinates (4, 5) it is 4 units from the vertical axis and 5 units from the horizontal axis.

Counting Back (URG Unit 2)
A strategy for subtracting in which students start from a larger number and then count down until the number is reached. For example, to solve $8 - 3$, begin with 8 and count down three, 7, 6, 5.

Counting Down (*See* counting back.)

Counting Up (URG Unit 2)
A strategy for subtraction in which the student starts at the lower number and counts on to the higher number. For example, to solve $8 - 5$, the student starts at 5 and counts up three numbers (6, 7, 8). So $8 - 5 = 3$.

Cube (SG Unit 18)
A three-dimensional shape with six congruent square faces.

Cubic Centimeter (cc) (URG Unit 16; SG Unit 16)
The volume of a cube that is one centimeter long on each edge.

Cup (URG Unit 16)
A unit of volume equal to 8 fluid ounces, one-half pint.

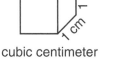
cubic centimeter

D

Decimal Fraction (URG Unit 15)
A fraction written as a decimal. For example, 0.75 and 0.4 are decimal fractions and $\frac{75}{100}$ and $\frac{4}{10}$ are called common fractions. (*See also* fraction.)

Denominator (URG Unit 13)
The number below the line in a fraction. The denominator indicates the number of equal parts in which the unit whole is divided. For example, the 5 is the denominator in the fraction $\frac{2}{5}$. In this case the unit whole is divided into five equal parts.

Density (URG Unit 16)
The ratio of an object's mass to its volume.

Difference (URG Unit 2)
The answer to a subtraction problem.

Dissection (URG Unit 12 & Unit 17)
Cutting or decomposing a geometric shape into smaller shapes that cover it exactly.

Distributive Property of Multiplication over Addition (URG Unit 19)
For any three numbers a, b, and c, $a \times (b + c) = a \times b + a \times c$. The distributive property is the foundation for most methods of multidigit multiplication. For example, $9 \times (17) = 9 \times (10 + 7) = 9 \times 10 + 9 \times 7 = 90 + 63 = 153$.

E

Equal-Arm Balance
See two-pan balance.

Equilateral Triangle (URG Unit 7)
A triangle with all sides of equal length and all angles of equal measure.

Equivalent Fractions (SG Unit 17)
Fractions that have the same value, e.g., $\frac{2}{4} = \frac{1}{2}$.

Estimate (URG Unit 5 & Unit 6)
1. (verb) To find *about* how many.
2. (noun) An approximate number.

Extrapolation (URG Unit 7)
Using patterns in data to make predictions or to estimate values that lie beyond the range of values in the set of data.

F

Fact Family (URG Unit 11; SG Unit 11)
Related math facts, e.g., $3 \times 4 = 12$, $4 \times 3 = 12$, $12 \div 3 = 4$, $12 \div 4 = 3$.

Factor (URG Unit 11; SG Unit 11)
1. In a multiplication problem, the numbers that are multiplied together. In the problem $3 \times 4 = 12$, 3 and 4 are the factors.
2. Whole numbers that can be multiplied together to get a number. That is, numbers that divide a number evenly, e.g., 1, 2, 3, 4, 6, and 12 are all the factors of 12.

Fewest Pieces Rule (URG Unit 4 & Unit 6; SG Unit 4)
Using the least number of base-ten pieces to represent a number. (*See also* base-ten pieces.)

Flat (URG Unit 4; SG Unit 4)
A block that measures 1 cm $\times$ 10 cm $\times$ 10 cm. It is one of the base-ten pieces that is often used to represent 100. (*See also* base-ten pieces.)

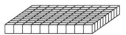

Flip (URG Unit 12)
A motion of the plane in which a figure is reflected over a line so that any point and its image are the same distance from the line.

Fraction (URG Unit 15)
A number that can be written as $\frac{a}{b}$ where a and b are whole numbers and b is not zero. For example, $\frac{1}{2}$, 0.5, and 2 are all fractions since 0.5 can be written as $\frac{5}{10}$ and 2 can be written as $\frac{2}{1}$.

Front-End Estimation (URG Unit 6)
Estimation by looking at the left-most digit.

G

Gallon (gal) (URG Unit 16)
A unit of volume equal to four quarts.

Gram
The basic unit used to measure mass.

H

Hexagon (SG Unit 12)
A six-sided polygon.

Horizontal Axis (SG Unit 1)
In a coordinate grid, the *x*-axis. The axis that extends from left to right.

I

Interpolation (URG Unit 7)
Making predictions or estimating values that lie between data points in a set of data.

J

K

Kilogram
1000 grams.

L

Likely Event (SG Unit 1)
An event that has a high probability of occurring.

Line of Symmetry (URG Unit 12)
A line is a line of symmetry for a plane figure if, when the figure is folded along this line, the two parts match exactly.

Line Symmetry (URG Unit 12; SG Unit 12)
A figure has line symmetry if it has at least one line of symmetry.

Liter (l) (URG Unit 16; SG Unit 16)
Metric unit used to measure volume. A liter is a little more than a quart.

M

Magic Square (URG Unit 2)
A square array of digits in which the sums of the rows, columns, and main diagonals are the same.

Making a Ten (URG Unit 2)
Strategies for addition and subtraction that make use of knowing the sums to ten. For example, knowing $6 + 4 = 10$ can be helpful in finding $10 - 6 = 4$ and $11 - 6 = 5$.

Mass (URG Unit 9 & Unit 16; SG Unit 9)
The amount of matter in an object.

Mean (URG Unit 5)
An average of a set of numbers that is found by adding the values of the data and dividing by the number of values.

Measurement Division (URG Unit 7)
Division as equal grouping. The total number of objects and the number of objects in each group are known. The number of groups is the unknown. For example, tulip bulbs come in packages of 8. If 216 bulbs are sold, how many packages are sold?

Measurement Error (URG Unit 9)
The unavoidable error that occurs due to the limitations inherent to any measurement instrument.

Median (URG Unit 5; DAB Unit 5)
For a set with an odd number of data arranged in order, it is the middle number. For an even number of data arranged in order, it is the number halfway between the two middle numbers.

Meniscus (URG Unit 16; SG Unit 16)
The curved surface formed when a liquid creeps up the side of a container (for example, a graduated cylinder).

Meter (m)
The standard unit of length measure in the metric system. One meter is approximately 39 inches.

Milliliter (ml) (URG Unit 16; SG Unit 16)
A measure of capacity in the metric system that is the volume of a cube that is one centimeter long on each edge.

Multiple (URG Unit 3 & Unit 11)
A number is a multiple of another number if it is evenly divisible by that number. For example, 12 is a multiple of 2 since 2 divides 12 evenly.

N

Numerator (URG Unit 13)
The number written above the line in a fraction. For example, the 2 is the numerator in the fraction $\frac{2}{5}$. (*See also* denominator.)

O

One-Dimensional Object (URG Unit 18; SG Unit 18)
An object is one-dimensional if it is made up of pieces of lines and curves.

Ordered Pairs (URG Unit 8)
A pair of numbers that gives the coordinates of a point on a grid in relation to the origin. The horizontal coordinate is given first; the vertical coordinate is given second. For example, the ordered pair (5, 3) tells us to move five units to the right of the origin and 3 units up.

Origin (URG Unit 8)
The point at which the *x*- and *y*-axes (horizontal and vertical axes) intersect on a coordinate plane. The origin is described by the ordered pair (0, 0) and serves as a reference point so that all the points on the plane can be located by ordered pairs.

P

Pack (URG Unit 4; SG Unit 4)
A cube that measures 10 cm on each edge. It is one of the base-ten pieces that is often used to represent 1000. (*See also* base-ten pieces.)

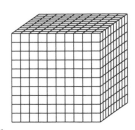

Palindrome (URG Unit 6)
A number, word, or phrase that reads the same forward and backward, e.g., 12321.

Parallel Lines (URG Unit 18)
Lines that are in the same direction. In the plane, parallel lines are lines that do not intersect.

Parallelogram (URG Unit 18)
A quadrilateral with two pairs of parallel sides.

Partitive Division (URG Unit 7)
Division as equal sharing. The total number of objects and the number of groups are known. The number of objects in each group is the unknown. For example, Frank has 144 marbles that he divides equally into 6 groups. How many marbles are in each group?

Pentagon (SG Unit 12)
A five-sided, five-angled polygon.

Perimeter (URG Unit 7; DAB Unit 7)
The distance around a two-dimensional shape.

Pint (URG Unit 16)
A unit of volume measure equal to 16 fluid ounces, i.e., two cups.

Polygon
A two-dimensional connected figure made of line segments in which each endpoint of every side meets with an endpoint of exactly one other side.

Population (URG Unit 1; SG Unit 1)
A collection of persons or things whose properties will be analyzed in a survey or experiment.

Prediction (SG Unit 1)
Using data to declare or foretell what is likely to occur.

Prime Number (URG Unit 11)
A number that has exactly two factors. For example, 7 has exactly two distinct factors, 1 and 7.

Prism
A three-dimensional figure that has two congruent faces, called bases, that are parallel to each other, and all other faces are parallelograms.

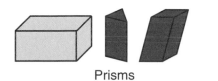

Prisms   Not a prism

Product (URG Unit 11; SG Unit 11; DAB Unit 11)
The answer to a multiplication problem. In the problem $3 \times 4 = 12$, 12 is the product.

Q

Quadrilateral (URG Unit 18)
A polygon with four sides.

Quart (URG Unit 16)
A unit of volume equal to 32 fluid ounces; one quarter of a gallon.

R

Recording Sheet (URG Unit 4)
A place value chart used for addition and subtraction problems.

Rectangular Prism (URG Unit 18; SG Unit 18)
A prism whose bases are rectangles. A right rectangular prism is a prism having all faces rectangles.

Regular (URG Unit 7; DAB Unit 7)
A polygon is regular if all sides are of equal length and all angles are equal.

Remainder (URG Unit 7)
Something that remains or is left after a division problem. The portion of the dividend that is not evenly divisible by the divisor, e.g., $16 \div 5 = 3$ with 1 as a remainder.

Right Angle (SG Unit 12)
An angle that measures 90°.

Rotation (turn) (URG Unit 12)
A transformation (motion) in which a figure is turned a specified angle and direction around a point.

Row (URG Unit 11)
In an array, the objects lined up horizontally.

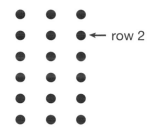

Rubric (URG Unit 2)
A written guideline for assigning scores to student work, for the purpose of assessment.

S

Sample (URG Unit 1; SG Unit 1)
A part or subset of a population.

Skinny (URG Unit 4; SG Unit 4)
A block that measures 1 cm $\times$ 1 cm $\times$ 10 cm. It is one of the base-ten pieces that is often used to represent 10. (*See also* base-ten pieces.)

Square Centimeter (sq cm) (SG Unit 5)
The area of a square that is 1 cm long on each side.

Square Number (SG Unit 11)
A number that is the product of a whole number multiplied by itself. For example, 25 is a square number since $5 \times 5 = 25$. A square number can be represented by a square array with the same number of rows as columns. A square array for 25 has 5 rows of 5 objects in each row or 25 total objects.

Standard Masses
A set of objects with convenient masses, usually 1 g, 10 g, 100 g, etc.

Sum (URG Unit 2; SG Unit 2)
The answer to an addition problem.

Survey (URG Unit 14; SG Unit 14)
An investigation conducted by collecting data from a sample of a population and then analyzing it. Usually surveys are used to make predictions about the entire population.

T

Tangrams (SG Unit 12)
A type of geometric puzzle. A shape is given and it must be covered exactly with seven standard shapes called tans.

Thinking Addition (URG Unit 2)
A strategy for subtraction that uses a related addition problem. For example, $15 - 7 = 8$ because $8 + 7 = 15$.

Three-Dimensional (URG Unit 18; SG Unit 18)
Existing in three-dimensional space; having length, width, and depth.

TIMS Laboratory Method (URG Unit 1; SG Unit 1)
A method that students use to organize experiments and investigations. It involves four components: draw, collect, graph, and explore. It is a way to help students learn about the scientific method.

Turn (URG Unit 12)
(*See* rotation.)

Turn-Around Facts (URG Unit 2 & Unit 11 p. 37; SG Unit 11)
Addition facts that have the same addends but in a different order, e.g., $3 + 4 = 7$ and $4 + 3 = 7$. (*See also* commutative property of addition and commutative property of multiplication.)

Two-Dimensional (URG Unit 18; SG Unit 18)
Existing in the plane; having length and width.

Two-Pan Balance
A device for measuring the mass of an object by balancing the object against a number of standard masses (usually multiples of 1 unit, 10 units, and 100 units, etc.).

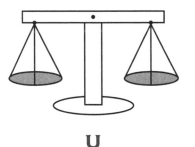

U

Unit (of measurement) (URG Unit 18)
A precisely fixed quantity used to measure. For example, centimeter, foot, kilogram, and quart are units of measurement.

Using a Ten (URG Unit 2)
1. A strategy for addition that uses partitions of the number 10. For example, one can find $8 + 6$ by thinking $8 + 6 = 8 + 2 + 4 = 10 + 4 = 14$.
2. A strategy for subtraction that uses facts that involve subtracting 10. For example, students can use $17 - 10 = 7$ to learn the "close fact" $17 - 9 = 8$.

Using Doubles (URG Unit 2)
Strategies for addition and subtraction that use knowing doubles. For example, one can find $7 + 8$ by thinking $7 + 8 = 7 + 7 + 1 = 14 + 1 = 15$. Knowing $7 + 7 = 14$ can be helpful in finding $14 - 7 = 7$ and $14 - 8 = 6$.

V

Value (URG Unit 1; SG Unit 1)
The possible outcomes of a variable. For example, red, green, and blue are possible values for the variable *color*. Two meters and 1.65 meters are possible values for the variable *length*.

Variable (URG Unit 1; SG Unit 1)
1. An attribute or quantity that changes or varies.
2. A symbol that can stand for a variable.

Vertex (URG Unit 12; SG Unit 12)
1. A point where the sides of a polygon meet.
2. A point where the edges of a three-dimensional object meet.

Vertical Axis (SG Unit 1)
In a coordinate grid, the *y*-axis. It is perpendicular to the horizontal axis.

Volume (URG Unit 16; SG Unit 16)
The measure of the amount of space occupied by an object.

Volume by Displacement (URG Unit 16)
A way of measuring volume of an object by measuring the amount of water (or some other fluid) it displaces.

W

Weight (URG Unit 9)
A measure of the pull of gravity on an object. One unit for measuring weight is the pound.

X

Y

Z